WEST HIGHLAND WALKS: THREE

HAMISH MacINNES

WEST HIGHLAND WALKS: THREE
ARRAN TO BEN LUI

'Pleasure is the outcome of exercise'
Motto of Clan MacInnes

HODDER AND STOUGHTON
LONDON SYDNEY AUCKLAND TORONTO

Acknowledgments

I am indebted to various people who checked the manuscript and contributed information, especially A. Garvie and R. Turner of Mull, Professor A. Hetherington, Professor M. MacDonald and Miss E. Whittome; and also my thanks go to Miss E. Brantley for conscientious assistance in both the fieldwork and the typing of the manuscript.

The satellite photograph is reproduced by permission of the United States Department of the Interior and the Brooch of Lorne photograph by permission of Graham MacDougall of MacDougall. Other photographs by Hamish MacInnes. Photographic artwork by Graeme Hunter.

British Library Cataloguing in Publication Data
MacInnes, Hamish
  West highland walks.
  3: Arran to Ben Lui
  1. Highlands (Scotland)—Description and
  travel—Guide-books
  I. Title
  914.11'804858   DA880.H7
  ISBN 0 340 26912 X

Contents

Introduction

THIS IS THE third volume in which I have tried to reflect a little of how I see these rugged, windswept Highlands. I am indebted for the years of sheer pleasure which their lochs, mountains and moorlands have given me; their solitude and the fascination of their history. In time one begins to assemble the jigsaw complexities of clan feuds and the pattern of life which evolved from the desolate glens—glens made increasingly desolate by the Clearances when sheep replaced families, and Highlanders, who had tilled their land and tended their beasts for centuries, were themselves herded like animals, driven to the shores to make way for sheep and told to 'fish or die'. From 1763 to 1775 20,000 people left for America alone; the majority of these were voluntary emigrants from the Highlands and Islands.

I have tried to portray with my camera the many and varied moods of the Western Highlands, including also the places of greatest historical interest. But my attempt must inevitably fall short of the ideal and I hope that readers will feel inclined to go and see for themselves; in so doing they will be amply rewarded.

Had I shared the view of Henry Ford who said "History is bunk", I should not have written anything at all. But out of consideration for his and similar opinions, I have kept the text concise and appreciate that many historical gaps must be spanned by the discerning reader, for whom there is fortunately a wide choice of literature.

Some people (obviously English) state that the two most consistent factors in the Scottish Highlands are the rain and the midges: true perhaps, at least for the midsummer visitor. Spring and autumn are usually the best and driest months to holiday in Scotland, spring being the most

◄ *A satellite photograph showing the area covered by this guide. The long peninsula, bottom centre, is Kintyre, with Arran on its right. Bottom left is Islay, with Jura above and Colonsay to its left. The Island of Mull is directly above this. (NASA photograph).*

favoured season, for though there may be snow on the tops in May, it complements the freshness of the glens and the sharpness of the air often gives desert-like clarity.

The area covered by this guide embraces the West Coast of Scotland between Arran and Mull, including all the territory as far east as Loch Lomond. The northern boundary of the guide meets up with Volume 1 in this series at Tyndrum to the east and Appin to the west. The selective visitor can choose any one part of a region which takes his or her fancy. To get to know Scotland, roads and cars should be left behind. Indeed, I sometimes find a vehicle can be a positive hindrance in some of the more out of the way places; it is often much easier to continue on foot than to return to a car.

Although there is no law of trespass in Scotland, and many of the old tracks are rights of way, it is better to ask permission before venturing over the hills and through the glens, especially during the stalking season which starts in September on most estates. But it is worth noting that land under the benevolent care of the National Trust for Scotland is not subject to any restrictions at such times.

In compiling this book I have attempted to cater for all degrees of energy expenditure, from the leisurely prospect of viewing a castle which entails a five-minute stroll from one's car, to long and strenuous walks into remote but rewarding recesses of the Western Highlands. Where possible I have included variations to walks which will enable a change of plan should the weather deteriorate and, with a bit of judicious map study on the part of the walker, other alternatives will become apparent. Having been fortunate enough to see the region covered in this book over a period of years in all sorts of weather, I have tried to present a balanced coverage of places of historical interest, together with walks in areas of scenic beauty. Beauty, however, is in the eye of the beholder and perhaps not many readers would agree with me when I say that the Rannoch Moor has a peculiar fascination in a winter's blizzard or that the naked peaks of Arran adopt a fresh charm in rain and mist.

Fortunately or unfortunately, depending on the way you look at it, some of the walks don't end at the same point as you started from. This may cause complications but I feel that this can add that bit of zest to the day's adventure and, after all, it would no longer be the wilds of Scotland if there was a shuttle service between lonely Highland glens.

As I have spent a considerable part of my career rescuing people from the hills and mountains of Scotland, I cannot stress too strongly the need for readers to take care on these moors and hills. The maps in this book show the routes of the walks described, but they are meant only for general placing reference, and walkers taking the longer hikes into secluded parts or mountainous areas should take a larger scale map with them as well. Sudden adverse weather may necessitate a change of plan, and here also a more detailed map becomes essential, as does a compass and, still more important, the ability to use both correctly.

The West Coast presents a complicated, loch-indented coastline, rather like a frayed cloth. The hills are relatively low, but they are also exposed to the wide Atlantic: wind and storm can blow up very quickly indeed, occasionally even bringing snow to the higher tops in summer. When venturing on to the mountains, be prepared with adequate clothing, a map, compass and spare food. The spring snow can linger into summer in north-facing corries and there are often frosts at this time of year. The snow surface can become very hard and correspondingly treacherous to the unwary. Therefore always choose your route according to prevailing conditions and the speed of the party. Since this book caters for such a wide age and fitness range, I have omitted any reference to time in respect of the various walks. As long as enough daylight is allowed for the return trip, without being too tired, any one of the expeditions should be safely within the capabilities of the average walker.

The West Highlands are crammed with history. In the distant past Mesolithic people, including the flint users who emigrated from Ireland to the Scottish mainland, moved northwards through this area, but left little evidence of their simple way of life. It was probably the Neolithic tribes who succeeded them who constructed the chambered cairns. They were a race of seafarers who came up the West Coast from the Mediterranean. The vitrified forts were built much later, during the Iron Age. Their pattern of distribution suggests that enemies approached from the east; the brochs, too, were of this period and were probably a development of the dun or fort. Brochs are only found in the north and west of Scotland; they are circular with very thick walls, sometimes up to twelve metres high, through which run galleries. Typically, the only entrance was a low narrow doorway. Brochs were possibly built as refuges against sea-raiders, or in defence against the 'Fort People' from the east.

The Picts first appear in history at the tail end of the third century AD. There are records of them fighting the Romans; so persistent was their harassment that the effective influence of the Roman Empire was pushed back to the Forth-Clyde boundary; later it receded even further south to Hadrian's Wall.

The Scots under Cairbre Riada established a kingdom in County Antrim in the third century called Dalriada (the Portion of Riada). It was about AD 258 that they began to settle in Argyll on the flat isthmus of Crinan. Their base was Dunadd, a natural fortress, and this kingdom also became known as Dalriada. However, it wasn't until 503 that they arrived in force and captured much of the mainland, as well as Islay. The kingdom approximated to the area of the county of Argyll. Scots moved over from Ireland in increasing numbers early in the sixth century. They were a Gaelic-speaking people who brought Christianity with them. In 563 Columba founded the Celtic Church which flourished for five centuries and, from his base in Iona, commenced the conversion of the Picts, travelling as far as the Pictish capital at Inverness to convert King Brude.

A great struggle ensued between the Picts and the Scots,

the latter being ultimately victorious, and in 843 Kenneth MacAlpin became the first King of Scotland. With the passage of time, and partly due to the influence of David I (1123–53), a division again became apparent in Scotland. He introduced feudalism by making grants of land, especially up the eastern coastal plain and along the Moray Firth. The Celtic, Gaelic-speaking people of the north and west bitterly opposed this Anglicisation, with the result that the geographical boundaries of the Highland Celt commenced with the mountains and embraced the Highland regions of Scotland. Here they developed as a separate people with their own language and culture, living under a totally different structure of society: the clan system. It was a family union, where the members were united under a chief, and each tribe or clan bore the same name.

The Norsemen came in a series of invasions and dominated the western seaboard for four centuries, but by the mid-thirteenth century the Scots had overrun the Viking colony of North Scotland and had occupied the Hebrides. The Vikings were finally defeated at the Battle of Largs in 1263, but they have left their mark in the place-names and culture of the Highlands.

The centuries following were times of anarchy. The Western Highlands were little influenced by the wars to the south—even the War of Independence in which starred the indomitable Bruce. Here was a warrior in the mould of Alexander who made Scottish history, much of it in the area covered by this guide, from Arran to the Pass of Brander. A hard man! It was an era of bloody deeds in the lawless Highlands, of repeated massacres and reprisals. A verse which holds more than a grain of truth tells that after God made the Highlander from horse droppings . . .

Quoth God to the Highlander, "What will you now?"
"I will go to the Lowland, Lord, and there steal a cow . . ."

After the fall of the Stewarts and the upsurge of Jacobitism, the Highlands again became ensnared in the web of Scottish politics. Clans had merged for mutual protection, giving birth to such powerful confederations as that of the MacDonalds under one supreme chief who, from about 1354, took the title of the Lord of the Isles.

Both James III and James IV did much to subjugate the unruly clansmen. Between 1493 and 1499 James IV sailed to Western Scotland six times and many Highlanders fought for him at Flodden; he had a smattering of the Gaelic which enhanced his popularity with the clansmen. The Campbells, under the Earls and later the Dukes of Argyll, always associated themselves with the Protestant Lowlands, inevitably becoming a hated and feared clan.

Despite the troubles, an oral culture survived and even prospered. Each chief had his bard who recorded events in song and verse. The bagpipe became the versatile instrument of both war and peace. During the seventeenth century and the early part of the eighteenth, the Highland scene was relatively peaceful and during this period lived some of the greatest poets: Duncan Ban MacIntyre, Alexander Macdonald and Rob Donn.

From time to time there were abortive attempts to win back the throne for the Stewarts, but the one with the most far-reaching effects proved to be the Jacobite Rising of 1745, which changed the course of Highland history, bequeathing an aftermath of misery and depredation. It now seems incredible that the adventurer, Prince Charles, could have rallied the clans as he did, arriving from France without money or arms, with a surplus only of confidence. What the young Prince lacked in pistols and louis d'or, he made up for in eloquence and personality. One is forced to admire his audacity and regret his final decline in exiled defeat: he eventually died an alcoholic.

The punitive measures employed against the Highlanders after the 'Forty-five were crushing indeed. Men loyal to the Crown fared little better than those with Jacobite sympathies. Wearing of Highland dress was prohibited and the penalty for simply playing the pipes could be transportation. The chiefs were deprived of all authority over their clans, whilst the Disarming Act forbade the carrying of weapons by the clansmen. Gaelic speech, too, was discouraged. These Acts above all caused the disintegration of the clans. Some of the laws were not rescinded for thirty years; others not at all.

The chiefs became lairds. There was a boom in cattle, so many of the chiefs either sold or leased their land to the highest bidder. The old way of life was totally disrupted and emigration increased. Then a series of famines occurred between 1768 and 1773: crops failed and the cattle died. The destitute people, clothed only in sacking, scoured the beaches for edible shellfish.

Later the cattle trade declined and, in the late eighteenth century, it was realised that sheep were better able to weather the Highland winters and provide an alternative. This discovery marked the beginning of the Clearances: people were thrown out of their houses, many of which were subsequently burned, and forced to move to the coast or emigrate. The sheep needed space . . . On one occasion a shipload of Camerons arrived in Sydney and a man, scanning the passenger list, was heard to exclaim, "Look here, the Camerons will soon be filling the country. Over two hundred of them have arrived on this one ship!"

People often wonder why the Highlanders accepted the Clearances so humbly—there was very little bloodshed. But the menfolk were away fighting in the Napoleonic Wars and the clergy, who wielded a powerful influence over the people, ignobly supported the lairds. Yet the Clearances were economically inevitable.

The decline in the Highlander's traditional way of life had a drastic effect on his outlook. The most enterprising travelled overseas; those who stayed were not helped by the rigid discipline of religion and suffered severe hardships. The numerous men who were evicted to the coast built hovels, fished and tried to raise crops without any security of tenure. They were at the mercy of the factors and the landowners, with no legal redress since the lairds were also the magistrates. At this time, in the late nineteenth century, dissatisfaction was growing. Deer forests and grouse moors had become fashionable for the rich and in some areas crofters were forbidden to repair leaking roofs with rushes or heather because the removal of the raw material might cause the grouse discomfort! Crops were eaten and trampled by marauding deer, but deer, to the common crofter, were untouchable.

The tinder was set alight at Braes in Skye when irate women forced police to burn an eviction notice. But the law returned, spurred on by an enraged Inverness magistrate. Sixty police under two sheriffs and officers arrived at Braes, close to Portree. The Battle of the Braes was fought with batons and stones. No lives were lost but a battered police posse limped back to Portree. Gladstone, who was Prime Minister at the time, was concerned. Warships were sent to the island and troops landed, but the population of Braes was unimpressed. Following this incident the government at last realised the injustices which the Highlanders were enduring; the result was the Crofters Holding Act of 1886, which gave the crofters security of tenure. Nowadays, the croft is too small a unit to be commercially viable and crofters usually hold another job as well. Inevitably, the young people move into the cities, seeking work, and the proportion of the elderly increases each year in crofting communities.

The discovery of oil has for the present given a fresh lease of life to the Highlands, and several new industries have been created; some, alas, accompanied by pollution. It is time people realised that Scotland's greatest heritage lies in its unspoiled scenery: seemingly unproductive wild tracts of country are its most valuable asset. Over the years the Highlands have scarcely altered; the old bridle path, the String of Lorn, is virtually the same as when MacCailean Mor was murdered on it by the MacDougalls in 1294. Let us hope that in the future this unique land will not be exploited beyond retrieval, but allowed to remain essentially a 'Wilderness' area within our nation.

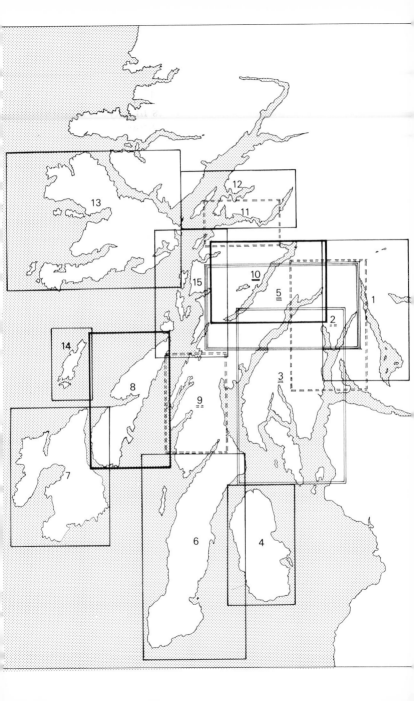

Loch Lomond to Crianlarich and Ben More

BY FAR THE most popular approach to the southern part of the Western Highlands is from Tarbet, Loch Lomond-side. Though the sinuous A82 which hugs the west bank of Loch Lomond can be a driver's nightmare on a holiday weekend, the loch itself is charming and offers varied and superb views both winter and summer, despite its proximity to the great industrial belt of the Clyde.

Before we cross over to Loch Long from Tarbet, let us briefly explore Loch Lomond-side and the continuing defile of Glen Falloch up to Crianlarich.

There are more than thirty islands in Loch Lomond. Twelve of the best are in the lower part of the loch where it swells from the spine of the west coast road with its stomach towards Balmaha at the south-east end. The first, from the bottom of the loch, is Inchmurrin (from St Mirren), with a tottering castle on its southerly shore, once the home of the Earl of Lennox. Part of the shore at Endrick Water, and five islands, form a 600-acre nature reserve, popular with the birds; many geese come here for their winter holidays. There is also an abandoned nunnery and church on the island of Inchcailloch.

Various clans had their homes round the loch. Of these only the Colquhouns survive as landowners. Others were the MacFarlanes and the MacGregors, whose popular hobbies were warring and cattle rieving. The moon was known as MacFarlane's lantern in honour of their nocturnal activities. The MacGregors were even worse and their master of banditry was infamous, Rob Roy MacGregor, Loch Lomond's Robin Hood. In 1603, just to the west of the lower end of the loch, the MacGregors butchered almost 300 Colquhouns in battle, and then ran riot, plundering throughout the countryside. After this, Old Man Colquhoun presented himself at Stirling before James VI with 220 widows, each displaying the bloody clothing of her husband on a pole. King James was understandably disturbed and outlawed the Clan Gregor, forfeiting their lands for keeps and even proscribing their name. But you

can't keep a bad clan down, and their way of life continued. In 1715, they sided with the Stewarts in the Jacobite Rising. For this adventure the Stewarts, who had outlawed the MacGregors a hundred years before, were themselves outlawed.

Loch Lomond is Britain's largest expanse of fresh water, stretching some twenty-seven square miles. As it is in the very backyard of Glasgow, it is justly popular for boating, fishing and its surrounding area for walking. Smoke, as from Indian encampments, spirals up from fires on the shore, for the Glaswegian likes his 'drum up', his cup of tea. There is good fishing in the loch and enormous pike; one was caught, weighing 33.5kg.

The east side of the loch is dominated by Ben Lomond, the Beacon Mountain (974m/3196ft). It can be climbed without difficulty, other than considerable energy expenditure, from Rowardennan, where a footpath starts. From Rowardennan Hotel there is also a fine forest walk, and a forest road and footpath continue north up the east bank of the loch as far as Glen Falloch, to Beinglas Farm. This route, fourteen miles of it, part of it the West Highland Way, starts by going north to Ptarmigan Lodge (public road, then forest road) and after two and a half miles, follows a branch road to the path by the loch. This continues north to Rowchoish and Inversnaid Hotel. There is sometimes a summer steamer service to Inversnaid as well as a ferry from near Inveruglas on the west shore.

Continuing northwards, in three-quarters of a mile, you pass Rob Roy's Cave, one of that infamous adventurer's safe hideaways. Robert the Bruce also had overnight accommodation in the cave in 1306 after he and his men had a tedious ferry operation across the loch in a small boat.

There is an old fort at the top of the hill road to Loch Arklet, to the east of Inversnaid. The fort, or garrison, was sacked twice by the MacGregors. After its third rebuilding it was under the command of General Wolfe (of Quebec fame) when he was a young officer.

◀ *Ben Lomond guarding the east shore of Loch Lomond.*

Beyond Rob Roy's Cave, the going is more difficult and it is better to keep above the Loch for about a mile, then drop again to the shore where there is a track. It's well marked. After this, climb over a big headland. Beyond Doune, go north to Ardleish on what is now a better path, then past Dubh Lochan over the bridge at Beinglas to the bridge over the River Falloch.

Following Glen Falloch a track goes up the Dubh Eas from Glenfalloch Farm to Glen Shira, which is described later from Inveraray. As the A82 climbs alongside the River Falloch you pass the Falls of Falloch about two miles beyond the farm. These are worth inspection, especially in spate.

Crianlarich is not the most beautiful place on earth and looks as if it has been assembled with debris from trains of the West Highland Line. Nevertheless, it is at the hub of a super area for fishing, walking and touring. From here the biggest mountains in the Southern Highlands rear up as if taking a deep breath from the green sea of Forestry Commission plantings, though the Forestry roads do give good access to some of the tops.

East of Crianlarich, on an islet at Loch Dochart, are the remains of an ancient castle. This is an old MacGregor stronghold. Just past the castle, at the end of a straight, is Benmore Farm. From close by, it's possible to climb Ben More (1174m/3850ft). Go east a short way along the road from the farm to a stile. From here follow the marked route. There is no difficulty in the ascent, and little of interest until the summit cairns stagger into view. The summit, however, offers fine panoramas—for these alone the slog is worthwhile.

The A82 west of Crianlarich follows Strath Fillan. Here, the River Fillan stems from the bowels of Ben Lui, first as the Rund and Allt Coire Laoigh streams, then the Rivers Cononish, Fillan, Dochart and finally the Tay.

Near where the main road crosses the river there is a

◄ *Loch Lomond and Ben Lomond, right of centre, from the A82. Across the loch left is Inversnaid.*

pool known as St Fillan's Pool, not half a mile up the valley from St Fillan's Priory. The pool was said to have had miraculous healing properties and the afflicted came great distances to be cured. The bones of the left arm of the saint were venerated for centuries. Before the Battle of Bannockburn they were paraded in front of Bruce's kneeling army by the Abbot of Inchaffray.

Bruce himself had a narrow escape in a battle about a mile from the pool. The site of this conflict between Bruce and John MacDougall, Lord of Lorne, is known as Dail Righ and is between the old bridge over the river and the Cononish track. What happened was that Bruce, who had been defeated by the English at Methven in 1306, hot-footed it up through Perthshire, to seek refuge with Campbell of Loch Awe. This part of his journey in Strath Fillan was the country of John MacDougall who had an old score to settle because Bruce had recently knifed MacDougall's father-in-law, Red Comyn, John of Badenoch, to death at the high altar of Greyfriars Church, Dumfries. Just to complicate matters further, other branches of the MacDougall clan were pro-Bruce.

Waiting at Dail Righ, John MacDougall had with him at least a thousand clansmen, which outnumbered Bruce's force about three to one. The rough terrain allowed Bruce's cavalry no advantage, and after a ding-dong battle, the King gave the order to retreat and personally led a brave rearguard action. There were a number of womenfolk in his party, including the Queen and Marjorie, his daughter. During this savage skirmish three of John MacDougall of Lorne's best warriors, which included the brave brothers MacIndrosser, 'the hardiest in the land', cut off the King's retreat and ambushed him in a narrow defile close to the small lochan, Lochan nan Arm. When Bruce was separated from his company, the first man seized the bridle, the second his leg and the other man leapt behind the King, grabbing his shoulder. Doubtlessly he was

Ben More and Stobinian from Strath Fillan, near Crianlarich.   ▶

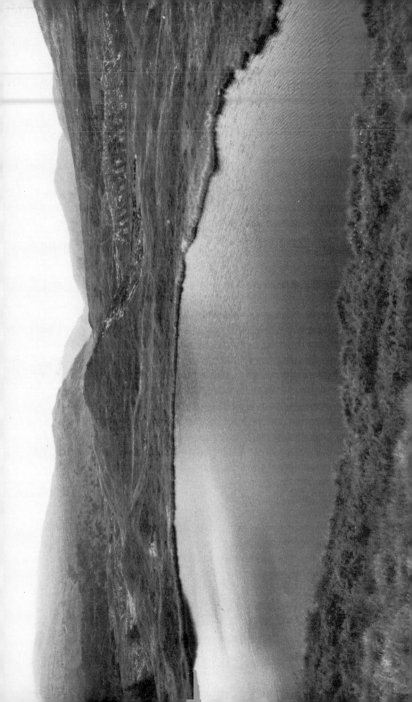

wearing armour or he wouldn't have survived this on-slaught. The man who had seized the bridle was given such a blow with Bruce's sword that both arm and shoulder were sliced from his body. Bruce then spurred his horse which dashed forward, dragging the assailant who held his leg. The man lost his footing and his hand jammed in the stirrup. As for the clansman who had leapt up behind Bruce, the King lifted him over his head onto the horse's neck and gave such a blow with the sword that the man's skull was cleft to the brain and he crashed to the ground a mess of blood. With one remaining blow, Bruce then killed the man he had dragged by the stirrup.

That was the stuff that adventure was made of in those days. John Barbour, who had eye-witness accounts of the battle, records the words of one of John of Lorne's own commanders, Baron MacNaughton: "Assuredly ye now behold retreating the starkest man of might that ever ye saw in your life. For yonder knight, by his doughty act and amazing manhood has slain in short space three men of great strength and pride and so dismayed all our host that no man dare go after him."

The man who had leapt behind Bruce had died grasping part of the King's surcoat, and on this was the famous brooch, later known as the Brooch of Lorne, which was handed to John of Lorne after the battle, little compensation for his escaped enemy. This large and beautifully worked silver ornament has possibly Middle-Eastern or European origins. It is still in the possession of the Lorne MacDougalls, but for security is now kept in London.

Tarbet westwards and Argyll's Bowling Green

TARBET MEANS A narrow neck of land between two stretches of water over which ships were dragged. There are a lot of Tarbets (or Tarberts) in the West Highlands. In

◀ *Lochan nan Arm near Tyndrum, where Robert the Bruce was ambushed by the MacDougalls.*

1263 King Haakon of Norway sent his son-in-law Magnus with two score ships up Loch Long, a sea loch, to Arrochar and from there Magnus and his men dragged some of the galleys overland to Tarbet on Loch Lomond and ravaged the settlements along the loch with fire and sword. At the end of September that same year, the Vikings fought the Scots at the decisive Battle of Largs. The Vikings lost the day, at least the land battle. In violent storms the wounded King Haakon retired to the Orkneys where he died in December. The Hebrides were ceded to Scotland in 1266.

▼ *The Brooch of Lorne.*

To return to Tarbet, one can't but be impressed with the view of the jagged Cobbler (881m/2891ft). This compact mini-mountain above Arrochar was the Mecca of rock climbers during the depression years of the early 1930s. Its mica schist offers wrinkles in lieu of holds, and the steepness of its crags guarantees the severity of routes. The mountain is really called Ben Arthur, and though dwarfed somewhat by loftier and more prodigious neighbours, it is an inspiring sight.

There are two alternative walking routes to gain the top of the Cobbler. After crossing the bridge over Loin Water at the head of Loch Long, take the road on the right as far as Succoth Farm. Gain the slopes above via a stile and reach a forest road above by a further stile. Now go left and after a few hundred metres go right up a path which slants round the hillside to the Allt a' Bhalachain (Buttermilk Burn). The path now leads towards the Cobbler, passing the famous Narnain Boulder and Shelter Stone. Here in harder times climbers slept overnight when climbing on the Cobbler and the Narnain Boulder provided gymnastic problems for the rock climbers. Beyond the boulders, cross the stream and follow the tributary on the left that comes out of the main corrie of the Cobbler.

The highest peak is the middle summit, the Cobbler, whilst the north peak is known as the Cobbler's Last. The south peak is sometimes known as Jean, the Cobbler's Wife. There is easy access to the north peak from the corrie between the centre and north peaks, but the final summit block of the main peak requires some rock climbing skill. Also the Cobbler's Wife should be left alone, for she is both difficult and dangerous to approach, except by rock climbers, whom she tolerates. It is also possible to gain the ridge between Jean and the Cobbler up the steep slope from the left-hand corrie, reaching the Cobbler summit via the path, thereby making the traverse of the Cobbler

The Cobbler summit is the centre peak with the South Peak to the left ▶
and the North Peak to the right. In the foreground is the Shelter
Stone, with the Narnain Boulder beyond.

by its north peak more varied. Descent should be by one or other of these routes back into the corrie.

There is an alternative approach to the Cobbler via the west side of the Buttermilk Burn on Loch Long-side. This route follows the burn to the boulders, but it is muddy.

There are also some fine lower level walks in the Arrochar region. One starts at the head of Loch Long, taking first the road on the east side of Loin Water, then the path to Inveruglas Water. Here the Hydro Board road can be taken to Loch Sloy. Now take the track from the dam along the west side of the loch to beyond its head to gain a further road which goes down the Kinglas Water to Butterbridge on the A83. Though there is a bus service back to Arrochar from here, the old road over the Rest and Be Thankful gives pleasant walking. This walk is some thirteen miles, and can be shortened by starting from Inveruglas on Loch Lomond-side or, alternatively, by simply cutting down Loin Water to Arrochar from this point.

It is also possible to walk from Arrochar (or better yet, from Ardgartan, a couple of miles down the west shore of Loch Long) to Lochgoilhead. Take the road south alongside Loch Long, then a forest road to Coilessan, then climb to Corran Lochan from Mark. From the lochan, travel north for one and a half miles, slant down to Stuckbeg and then along the shore road to Lochgoil.

A more direct route takes the Coilessan Glen from the shore of Loch Long due west over the ridge (503m/1650ft) to follow down Donich Water to Lochgoilhead.

This rough peninsula between Loch Goil and Loch Long is sometimes called Argyll's Bowling Green. Rougher terrain is hard to find, but the name is derived from the Gaelic Buaile na Greine, meaning Sunny Cattle Fold, an old grazing area at Mark on Loch Long.

The B828 south to Lochgoilhead runs from the summit of the Rest and Be Thankful to a higher point (300m/983ft)

◀ *Jean, the Cobbler's Wife, the South Peak from the access path leading to the main summit.*

before contouring round Ben Donich. Another road with easier gradients runs from Loch Fyne through Hell's Glen. This route is lower (219m/719ft), though not so convenient of access from the east.

The area round Lochgoilhead is now rather congested with Forestry Commission conifers, chalets and caravans; yet the village, which bears the same name as the loch, retains much of its charm. The loch itself is one of the finest in Argyllshire. As well as the walks mentioned starting from Ardgartan, there are several forest walks on the east side of the village and also from Lettermay, a mile or so down the west side of the loch. The road down the west side ends at Carrick Castle and hamlet.

The castle dates from the fifteenth century and the walls are still intact. Carrick was probably built as a Lamont stronghold and was later a hunting seat for the Stewart kings, possibly James IV. In those days wild boar were plentiful and indeed the last boar killed in Britain was in nearby Cowal in 1690. The Argyll Campbells became the hereditary keepers of the castle and it withstood a Cromwellian siege in 1651. In 1685 its keeper was called to Edinburgh to answer questions on his chief's support of Monmouth's rebellion. In his absence, Atholl 'visited' the castle and plundered it, taking many sheep, horses and cattle. The castle wasn't restored after this attack.

A route of some eleven miles runs from Carrick Castle to Ardentinny, further down Loch Long-side. Take the path to Ardnahein, then continue along the shore to a point a quarter of a mile south-east of Toll nam Muc. Now climb to an ill-defined path through the forest which in turn meets a Hydro-electric access road on the Knap Burn. Here there is a seventy-five-metre electricity pylon (the wires span Loch Long). From Knap take a forest road, parallel with the shore to Ardentinny. Because the forest path becomes hard to find beyond the Knap Burn road, some find it easier to do this walk from south to north.

Carrick Castle, Loch Goil, probably built as a hunting seat for the ▶
Stewart kings.

Two further walks are worth mentioning, one to Strachur on Loch Fyne and the other to Whistlefield on Loch Eck. These are described later from those respective places.

The road over the Rest and Be Thankful appears to give a sigh of relief as it dips down to the tranquillity of Loch Fyne. Before the loch the road forks, the A83 encircling the head of Loch Fyne to gain Inveraray, and the A815 branching left to run eventually to the toe of Cowal. Less than a mile from the Glen Kinglas turn-off, a loop of the old road winds down to the tiny village of Cairndow. Keats stayed at the inn here last century after a hike across the Rest and Be Thankful. His name is diamond-scratched on a bedroom window pane. Nearby is Kilmorich Church, built in 1816 on thirteenth-century foundations. The church is hexagonal with a square tower. A similar and even better example of this construction can be seen at Dalmally, near the top of Loch Awe.

Ardkinglas House is situated in wooded parkland south and west of Cairndow. It was here in 1692 that MacIan, Chief of the Glencoe MacDonalds, belatedly came to take the Oath of Allegiance to the Crown at the hand of Sir Colin Campbell on the eve of the Massacre of Glencoe. There was once a castle on the site, but now there is no trace of this. Both house and gardens are usually open to the public during April and May under Scotland's Garden Scheme. The proceeds go to charity.

The principal village on the east coast of Loch Fyne is Strachur, and from here a sporting walk crosses the peninsula to Lochgoilhead, a distance of some nine miles. Turn east off the A815, following at first the sign for the Forest Walk. After just over a mile the road runs close to the River Cur. Where it bears north-east to Succoth Farm (not to be confused with Succoth above Arrochar) take the right-hand fork and go along the forest road in a south-easterly direction for a mile and follow the march fence up the glen to the Bealach an Lochain, past Curra Lochain to gain the Lettermay Burn to the road.

The hexagonal church at Kilmorich, upper Loch Fyne.   ▶

Bute and the three fingers of Cowal

SIX MILES SOUTH-WEST of Strachur is Castle Lachlan, still owned by the MacLachlans who have held it and the land for seven centuries. The name Lachlan means Norseman, and as the older castle is on the site of a Norse settlement it is possible they had formerly intermarried with the Vikings. There are two castles, the early one is perched on a rocky knoll which was protected by both moat and marshland. It is still more or less intact, but in need of first aid. The younger castle is half a mile to the east and dates from the mid-fifteenth century, with a double rectangular keep and a narrow open court between. It is not however open to the public. In 1746 the castle sustained a naval attack, as the chief supported Bonnie Prince Charlie. He was later killed at Culloden and it is said that his horse found its way back to Strathlachlan and swam across the loch to make the derelict castle vault its home. (It is interesting to note that in the 1950s a similar incident occurred when a horse swam from the castle across Loch Fyne to be found near Furnace.)

The clan has its own pet brownie who is supposed to take care of the family's fortunes. It obviously shared with many Scots of the time in a dislike for the Campbells. When one of the chief's sons married a Campbell, the brownie is reputed to have removed the entire wedding feast from the large banqueting hall.

The lochside road (B8000) continues to Otter Ferry, but the ferry no longer operates. The road striking east from Otter Ferry offers fine views, indeed some of the best in the whole area and it reaches a height of 300m. There is a chambered cairn near the summit. From here Loch Fyne is seen as a foreground to the Hebrides on a good day. Beyond Otter Ferry the road continues south to arrive at Tighnabruaich on the shores of the Kyles of Bute, while a minor continuation south from Millhouse ends at

◄ *The elder Castle Lachlan. The mid-fifteenth-century castle is half a mile to the east.*

Ardlamont Point, a great grassy headland fingering into the Sound of Bute where four big waterways reach out to various points of the compass: Kilbrannan Sound, between Arran and Kintyre, the Firth of Clyde, Loch Fyne and the Kyles of Bute.

A forest road runs north from Ardlamont House, close to the point, past Glenahuil to Rubha Mor Kames which is just south of Kames. This walk, which is about three and a half miles, goes through the Tighnabruaich Forest.

Tighnabruaich is one of the most picturesque villages on mainland Argyll. The name means house on the edge of the bank. It is a yachting paradise with the confines of the Kyles of Bute close at hand and the waiting open seaways.

For those more inclined to have their feet firmly on terra firma, a track goes north-west from the village crossing the Craignafeoch Burn to gain Acharosson Farm in about six miles.

From Tighnabruaich, a further walk follows the coast to Ormidale at the head of Loch Riddon, and on the way there is a well laid out forest trail of over a mile opposite Eilean Dubh. Nothing now remains of Glen Caladh Castle at this point, but further north, Eilean Dearg has the ruins of a prominent Campbell stronghold.

North of Loch Riddon is a fork where the Otter Ferry road comes in on the left. Beyond this the A8003 reaches a T-junction. To the left the A886 runs north through Glen Daruel, and if this is your way, it is worth looking at the old bridge over the River Ruel at the lower reach of the glen. Here in 1110 a battle was fought between the Viking son of Magnus Barefoot and the Scots. The Scots were

◄◄ *The Kyles of Bute, with Tighnabruaich beyond the second point right.*

◄ *The River Ruel, Glen Daruel. Here the Scots beat Magnus Barefoot's Vikings in 1110 and threw the corpses into the river, renamed the Bloody Water.*

The Island of Bute from the road to the north of Tighnabruaich.   ►

victorious and threw the corpses of the butchered enemy into the Ruel, which at one time was called Ruadh-thuil, Red Water, from the peaty colour. After the battle it became Ruith-fhuil, the Bloody Water, and anglicised as Glen Daruel.

The A886 running south from the T-junction skirts the edge of Loch Riddon to the narrows of the Kyles of Bute. These narrows are created by the Burnt Islands, a group of stepping-stone islets with a crew-cut of stunted trees and heather. There is a regular steamer service through these narrows, though it is further south at Colintraive (the Strait for Swimming) where the real narrows are located. Here the cattle were swum by drovers in former years. Colintraive is the car ferry point for Bute.

In contrast to nearby Arran, Bute is a lowland island. It is a mere sixteen miles long by four wide, tapering at the ends, and thereby offering only two coastlines, east and west. Its northern end seems almost jammed into the Kyles of Bute, whilst the southerly reaches out towards the island of Little Cumbrae in the Firth of Clyde. Bute's Garroch Head is a milestone for mariners entering or leaving the firth. Here is the Clyde's most fertile island. The highest point is Windy Hill (278m/911ft). It is a pleasant hill walk from the B8000.

Port Bannatyne would not win any prizes as a model town, nevertheless it does have certain attractions and is popular with yachting people who wish to avoid the steamer bustle of busier Rothesay. It has an unusual golf course with only thirteen holes; purists have to replay the last five.

The castle of Kames to the north-west of the village at the head of Kames Bay is a holiday centre for the Scottish Council for the Care of Spastics. The great square tower still stands intact, dating from the fourteenth century. Scotland's most renowned drinking vessel, the Bannatyne Mazer, is reputed to have been made here by John

◄ *Rothesay Castle, Bute, a remarkable fortress in the heart of the town.*

Bannatyne, the laird and also Keeper of Rothesay Castle. It was made to celebrate the stay of Robert the Bruce at Rothesay Castle in 1314, the year of the Battle of Bannockburn, when Bruce's daughter, Marjorie, was betrothed to Walter the Steward. From this union came the Stewart Kings. The title, Duke of Rothesay, is now taken by the heir to the thrones of England and Scotland.

Rothesay is the principal town of Bute and, like Brodick on Arran, developed through the early part of the century as a traditional Glasgow holiday resort. It is still popular and served with a reasonable steamer service from Wemyss Bay on the Renfrewshire coast. The Colintraive ferry plies to Rhubodach, little more than a long stone's throw across the Kyles, and from here an agreeable walk can be made round the northern tip of the island, offering fine views across the Kyles of Bute and north-west to Tighnabruaich.

Rothesay Castle is well worth spending some time browsing over, being one of the most important medieval castles in Scotland, and it combines both Celtic and Norman designs. About 300 metres back from Rothesay Pier, it is well hidden from the seafront. The principal structure is an enormous circular moated curtain wall of pink and grey sandstone. Four great circular towers project from the wall. A replica of the original bridge spans the moat on the north side (the original timbers were found in the moat). The bridge leads directly into the fore-tower, or donjon, built by James IV.

Rothesay Castle first appears in records in 1230, but the foundation date is more likely to have been 1156, which was the year that Somerled, together with his three sons, defeated the Vikings. In 1263 King Haakon held Rothesay Castle on his invasion of the Clyde and, after his defeat at Largs, it reverted to the King of Scots. Over the years that followed, the castle had a turbulent history and changed hands in Bruce's war with England. Its final demise as a stronghold came in the Monmouth rebellion of

St Blane's Chapel, Island of Bute, with its two-tier segregated graveyard, and Arran on the horizon. ▶

1685, when Campbell of Argyll attacked it without success, but several days later his brother took over and, in a surprise attack, the castle was sacked and burned. It was never again used for warring purposes. Now it is in the care of the Ministry of Works. The castle water supply was from the moat, supplied by Loch Fad. At one time there were several buildings within the curtain walls but now the only one remaining is the Chapel of St Michael the Archangel, patron saint of warriors. The remains of the Bloody Stair still exist between the chapel and the curtain wall. On these stairs in 1230 the High Steward's daughter plunged a dagger into her heart rather than fall victim of the Norsemen, after seeing her brother and father hacked to pieces below.

At Dunagoil Bay just a mile up the west coast from Garroch Head are the remains of a prehistoric vitrified fort. That means the stonework is fused together by means of fire. The vitrification takes place when wood, kelp and peat are fired in conjunction with a strong wind to form a fusion of siliceous rock-rubble. As the fuel contains both soda and sand, a slag-cement is created which greatly strengthened defensive walls. The best surviving example in Argyll is at Carradale in Kintyre. About fifty of these forts have been discovered in Scotland and a few in England, dating from the mid-British Iron Age. Access to the Dunagoil Bay fort is via a field gate to the cove which is a mere 200 metres from the road. The bay is superb with pink sand and the fort is on the south side on a flat-topped hill protected by fifteen-metre cliffs. It was occupied for at least 200 years between 100 BC and AD 500 and has been excavated on several occasions and various relics have been unearthed.

As you walk round the southerly tip of Bute, St Blane's Chapel is worth a visit. It is signposted from Garrochty Farm, some 400 metres off the road. The chapel itself is secluded in a grassy hollow on top of a tree-clad hillock.

The Island of Arran from Garrochty, Bute. The rock outcrop right is ▶
the site of an early fort.

Go through a gate to gain a farm road and, instead of following it, go left on a footpath by a wall which leads through a field and gates to the chapel. The Vikings destroyed the original building in 798. The present ruins date from the eleventh and twelfth centuries, and the Norman arch plus the two gables still stand. Just a few yards south-west of the arches lies the ruin of a cell said to be that of St Blane. Nearby are ninth-century Celtic stones. The Devil's Cauldron is a circular enclosure of huge stones close to the chapel. According to tradition it is supposed to have been a place of penance for confessed sinners.

The chapel graveyard is unusual, for men and women are segregated. It is said that this came about when the graveyard was being made and consecrated soil was being transported from Rome—ultimately by creel. It is related that a creel carrying-band broke and the foreman Abbot asked one of the women to lend her belt as a substitute. When she refused (possibly because she didn't want to lose her skirt), the irate Abbot ordered that the graveyard should be constructed in two tiers with females henceforth relegated to the lower level. After the Reformation this male chauvinism was relaxed and a few women have been accommodated in the higher lairs.

The most easterly prong of the Cowal trident of peninsulas is the most important, with Dunoon the principal town, connected to the Rest and Be Thankful by the A815 running north. Loch Striven forms its western boundary, approached by the B836. Despite being so close to Dunoon, Loch Striven has an air of remoteness. There is a walk of about four miles down the east shore from the head of the loch to Glenstriven House. This track is a public footpath which meets up with the Port Lamont road a short way beyond Glenstriven House. The lower reaches of Loch Striven are somewhat marred by a NATO refuelling base just north of Port Lamont and also by the evidence of an oil platform yard at Ardyne Point, costing many millions. Three concrete oil platforms were built here. It is now used for shipping timber from Argyll to Norway. There is a bus service between Port Lamont and Dunoon for those wanting to complete a round trip the easy way.

Closer to Dunoon a walk of twenty miles, starting north of Sandbank, takes one to Loch Striven. Follow the B836 Tighnabruaich road for a mile to the side road close to the Little Eachaig bridge. Now walk south up Glen Kin to the top. Here, go south-west over the Bealach na Sreine, then descend the Inverchaolain Glen to Loch Striven. Travel north along the shoreline via Inververgain to Ardtaraig. Buses also operate to Ardtaraig.

Dunoon is a tourist processing town. At least it caters for all aspects of visitor needs from paddling to putting. It is also a good centre from which to visit the hinterland of Cowal. The town extends round a double bay, the East and West, separated by the low ridge of Castle Hill whereon lie the remains of Dunoon Castle. The point of this ridge boasts a pier originally constructed by Robert Louis Stevenson's father. The lower slope of Castle Hill is adorned by the statue of Highland Mary, who gazes pensively towards the Ayrshire coast where she and Robert Burns were lovers. Mary Campbell, as she was called, was born in nearby Auchmore Farm. She met Burns when she entered service at Montgomery in Ayrshire. They exchanged Bibles over running water, a Scottish marriage rite. Later she died of a fever. Burns was heart-broken by her death. Here is an extract from his poem, 'Highland Mary':

> Wi' monie a vow, and lock'd embrace,
>   Our parting was fu' tender;
> And, pledging aft to meet again,
>   We tore oursels asunder;
> But oh! fell death's untimely frost,
>   That nipt my flower sae early!
> Now green's the sod, and cauld's the clay,
>   That wraps my Highland Mary!

O pale, pale now, those rosy lips,
  I aft hae kiss'd sae fondly!
And closed for ay the sparkling glance,
  That dwelt on me sae kindly!
And mould'ring now in silent dust,
  That heart that lo'ed me dearly!
But still within my bosom's core
  Shall live my Highland Mary.

There is little left today to mark the importance of Dunoon Castle. The spot has been fortified since the early days of the Dalriadic kingdom in the fourth century, and its turbulent and bloody history mainly concerned the Lamonts, who owned the land, and the nefarious Campbells. In 1563, Mary Queen of Scots stayed at the castle when on a visit to her sister who had married the fifth Earl of Argyll. In 1646, the Campbells lived up to their reputation of intrigue and treachery. In those days the seat of the Clan Lamont was Toward Castle, some seven miles south of Dunoon. When the eighth Earl of Argyll failed to besiege it, he suggested a truce which the Lamont chief accepted and withdrew his defences. The Campbells then surprised them, took the castle, laid waste the land and returned to Dunoon with hundreds of prisoners. They hanged thirty-six important members of the Lamont clan from a single tree on Castle Hill and massacred everyone else. In 1685, Murray of Atholl burned the castle. It was never restored.

There is a popular walk going up into the hilly ground above the town to Bishop's Glen. The path goes round the reservoir in the glen.

Three glens open out from the top of Holy Loch. Before exploring them it is worth visiting a curiosity in nearby Kilmun graveyard, near the Nuclear Submarine Base of

The statue of Highland Mary looks towards the Ayrshire coast from ▶
Dunoon. In the background is the pier and the Gourock–Dunoon car ferry.

the Holy Loch. Close to the west door of the ruined Collegiate Church are two interesting iron frames which were used in the early nineteenth century to secure coffin lids, thereby thwarting potential body-snatchers. The ivy-enveloped ruin was the first recorded Christian church in the area, founded by St Mun, a younger contemporary of St Columba. He is remembered by the village of Kilmun, and also by his crosier, which was held by a hereditary custodian until the sixteenth century.

Those visitors to the shores of Holy Loch who may speculate uneasily on the inscription on some of the tombstones in this graveyard, reading 'Free for a blast' should know it is the motto of Clan Clark, who, at one time, owned the land surrounding Loch Eck. Their chief, when entertaining James IV on a hunting expedition, saw his own hounds outrun the King's dogs and blew a blast on his hunting horn to call them off, thereby allowing the King's dogs to close in and bring the stag down. The King was so impressed by his host's generosity that he declared, "Henceforth, you are freed of all taxes." Thus the motto 'Free for a blast' was born.

The glen running left from the top of Holy Loch, Glen Lean, carries the road westwards to Loch Striven. The centre one, Glen Massan, runs deeply into the ramparts of the Beinn Mhor range and the last leads up to Loch Eck.

From upper Glen Massan, Beinn Mhor (741m/2430ft) can be ascended by taking the southerly nose leading onto Sron Mhor and following the ridge to Beinn Mhor's summit. Glen Massan is one of the highlights of Cowal.

For those interested in rhododendrons, the eighty-five acres of the Younger Botanical Gardens are a must, situated a mile south of Loch Eck. The Younger family bought Benmore Estate in 1891 and gave it to the Forestry Commission in 1925. It was during this time that H. G. Younger built up the collection of plants. They now come

The old church of Kilmun, Holy Loch, so named for its early Christian associations. Note the iron frames against the wall to frustrate body snatchers, and the atomic submarine in the loch. ▶

under the care of the Royal Botanic Gardens of Edinburgh. More than 200 species of rhododendron are represented here. The avenue of redwoods leading to Benmore House is the best example in the west of Scotland, each tree being more than thirty-six metres high. Benmore House is now used as an Outdoor Education Centre for Lothian Regional Council. There are many forest walks in the area round Benmore, and these are well marked and suitable for post-prandial excursions. One of these is Puck's Glen on the Dunoon road, less than a mile from Benmore. Despite its unpromising name, Puck's Glen is worth visiting, a pleasant walk through pine, larch and redwood. Eventually, the path reaches a hilltop, then wanders with many diversions over rustic bridges and mini-waterfalls; a delightful place on a fine day.

Many of us regard with dismay the acquisition of land, the exclusion of views and other restrictive practices imposed by the Forestry Commission. Yet one can't deny that many of the roads they have constructed offer access to areas which otherwise would have been difficult to visit, and also provide delectable walks to those not regarding themselves as hill-bashers and mountaineers. The long walk up the west bank of Loch Eck is one of these, and in seventeen miles one can reach Strachur. It is possible to take a bus to Benmore road-end and go north up Strath Eachaig to gain the Benmore Forest via the main gate of the Younger Botanical Gardens. Turn right to the lochside and follow the west bank of Loch Eck all the way up to Glenbranter.

On the Benmore–Strachur walk a diversion to the Paper Cave is worth making. The cave was used to secrete important Campbell papers during times of crises, especially upon the invasion of Murray of Atholl in 1685. It is situated on the lower slopes of Clach Bheinn, on the southerly wooded entrance of Coire an t-Sith (pronounced Corrantee). It was in this coire that 'Free for a Blast' Clan Clark were granted their short-lived immunity from taxes by James IV. The cave is marked on OS maps and for those equipped with a torch and willing to get dishevelled, it is possible to enter the inner chamber. An island offshore was used by Campbell's agent as a staging post. This gave him time to study the shore to ensure that he wasn't observed approaching the cave.

There is a six-mile walk from Craigbrack on the east side of Loch Eck to Lochgoilhead. Though it is rough going in places, it is a good cross-country route. Follow a path on the right up Coire Ealt through the plantings to reach the bealach (or saddle) between Beinn Bheula (779m/2557ft) and Cnoc na Tricriche. Now go down to the west side of Lochain nan Cnaimh, skirt round and keep to the right side of the Lettermay Burn (rough in places) to reach a forest road high above the burn. Follow down to Loch Goil.

Doon the watter to Arran

ONE GETS THE impression that the Isle of Arran is misplaced; as if on a dark night the Scottish Tourist Board towed it south to its present anchorage between the outspread arms of the Firth of Clyde in an attempt to entice tourists to visit a truly West Highland island in a more tranquil climate. Arran has all the vital statistics of the Western Highlands with mountain bog, moor and idyllic bays. It even has the highland midge and, if you go at the wrong time of year, abundant rain too. It has historic ruins and romantic history. I have a schoolboy's memories of Arran as the place where Robert the Bruce took note of the acrobatics of a diligent spider.

Arran is also a playground for leisure and recreation. Apart from reliable snow conditions for winter sports, it has everything from hill walks par excellence to several golf courses. Geared for the tourist, Arran has some hundred hotels and boarding houses, plus 300 cottages offering a variety of accommodation. There are also numerous camp-sites and several youth hostels. As well as the sports associated with the hills, Arran offers thriving

sea angling and sailing, water skiing and bathing. As the 40° isotherm passes through Arran, it is seldom cold and June is the driest month, with the most sun.

The island is a cornucopia of standing stones and ancient monuments and these are fun to browse over on off-days, or when the body or spirit is not willing to propel one to the glens and bens.

In prehistoric times, Arran was on the route by which immigrants made their way in short hops up the western seaboard of Britain. These first immigrants were most probably mesolithic sailor-hunter-fishermen. (It was the Momarine of the second-century geographer, Ptolemy.) From about 500 BC, Celtic immigrants followed. The last of these, the Scots, came from the Kingdom of Dalriada in Northern Ireland and towards the end of the fourth century AD established a twin kingdom bearing the same name in the area of the present counties of Argyll and Bute. They took with them the Christian religion and the Gaelic language and later gave Scotland its present name.

Arran was under Viking domination for four centuries, as were the Western and Northern Isles. The natural harbour of Lamlash became an important base for Viking operations.

Somerled, who was of Scots-Norwegian blood, established a breakaway Kingdom of the Isles which was roughly the size of Dalriada. By 1269, three years after the Battle of Largs, Norway sold the Western and Northern Isles of Scotland and by this time the Kingdom of the Isles was being absorbed into the wider kingdom of Scotland anyhow. The MacDonalds, descendants of Somerled, still tried to hold on to Arran, despite a counter claim on Arran and Bute by a Norman, Alexander, the High Steward (later Stewart), who had married a grand-daughter of Somerled's son Angus. With the might of the Crown behind him, Alexander won the struggle and Brodick Castle was established as a strategic Stewart base.

With the exception of a short period during the Scottish Wars of Independence, the Stewarts held Arran. Robert the Bruce created a Stewart Lord of Knapdale and Arran after his victory at Bannockburn. Arran will for ever be linked with this greatest of Scottish warrior kings. Before his descent on Arran, Bruce spent a winter on the island of Rathlin where he was concealed by Angus Og, Lord of the Isles. Angus was later to contribute 10,000 men to Bruce's campaign on the mainland of Scotland. Bruce crossed to Arran in the spring of 1306 with thirty-three galleys. Good Sir James Douglas had already surprised and seized Brodick Castle which was formerly held for King Edward of England. In Sir Walter Scott's *Lord of the Isles*, Bruce is reported to have sent an emissary called Cuthbert from Arran to the mainland at Turnbury, where his own castle stood. Cuthbert was briefed to signal at night by fire if the situation was conducive to an invasion of the mainland. When Bruce saw a fire on the given night he set sail from the promontory still called Kingscross. Arriving at Turnbury he discovered that it wasn't the prearranged signal which he had seen; nevertheless, the die was cast as far as he was concerned and his subsequent campaign against tremendous odds provides one of the great sagas of Scottish history. It is well documented in *The Bruce* by the fourteenth-century historian, John Barbour.

Sir Walter Scott must have felt Brodick Castle a more romantic setting than Kildonan Castle, which is the most likely firewatching viewpoint for Bruce to have chosen, for this castle is directly across the water from Turnbury. From Brodick Castle it is impossible to see Turnbury, due to intervening hills and the ponderous bulk of Holy Island.

In the fifteenth century the Boyd family obtained possession of the island when one of them wed Mary, a sister of James III. The Hamiltons took over when Mary was divorced and married Lord Hamilton who became Earl of Arran.

In 1786 an attempt was made to abolish the Celtic runrig system of field management, which had come through the Viking period unscathed. The change involved the abolition of common grazings and around a hundred communal farms, each of which supported about ten families. The new system proposed by John Burrel was to have divided the communal farms into 250 holdings, thereby depriving 750 families of access to the land which they had held for generations. The scheme proved unworkable and caused great distress on the island. People were herded to the coast where they were told to fish and grow potatoes. When the sheep moved in with the clearance of the glens, emigration was one of the few courses of action left to many of the people of Arran who went to the industrial towns of the mainland and to Canada. Many from the westerly glens went to Chaleur Bay, New Brunswick, and those from the north of the island to Quebec.

Later, Arran, on the very doorstep of Scotland's greatest industrial belt, inevitably became a tourist centre and, with the development of steamboat and rail links, 'doon the watter' became an annual pilgrimage for the masses, before the advent of foreign package holidays. Today Arran is more restful than it was in the 'thirties and one can fully enjoy the freedom of this delectable island.

The island is kidney-shaped and encircled by a fifty-six-mile highway, the A841. There are also two roads which cut across the island known as the Ross and the String. These run from Lamlash and Brodick respectively to the west side of the island. The Forestry Commission has also penetrated many of the glens with new roads, which are excellent for walking on wet days when the moorland is too squelchy. As well as being renowned for its butterflies (the Arran Brown is its own species), the island is famed for its red deer herds in the north. Arran seed potatoes, too, are world famous, as is Arran Dunlop cheese.

Arran still has reasonable communication with the mainland and steamers to Brodick operate from Ardrossan and sometimes from Wemyss Bay in summer. There is also a summer only car ferry from Claonaig to Lochranza at the north end of the island.

Brodick Castle, former seat of the Dukes of Hamilton and

Earls of Arran, is seen to its best advantage with Goat Fell as a backdrop. It is now the property of the National Trust for Scotland and open to visitors. One can still discern the ditches of the old Pictish fort, and the room and table used by Bruce are on view. There is the rather unusual feature of two turnpike stairs rising in two linked towers. At the eastern end there is a lower battery for cannon built by Cromwellian troops who occupied the castle in 1652. The Earl of Arran ambushed Cromwell's forces near Sannox, killed every soldier and thereby gained possession of the castle. The structure was added to in 1844 and the modern part contains fine furnishings and a handsome picture collection. Two gardens enhance the property: the flower and rose gardens go back to 1710 and the large woodland garden, renowned for its rhododendrons, was laid out in 1923.

For the young at heart, bicycles and mopeds can be hired in Brodick and for those wishing to walk or hill-climb, open country is but a short step away.

Goat Fell (874m/2866ft) is the highest peak on the island. The mountains are the remains of a dome of very coarse crystalled granite, which for the rock climber offers wonderful friction. The glens are particularly suited for walking.

Going north from Brodick on the A851, we skirt round the base of the Goat Fell massif and make our way to Corrie, a snug little village and indeed one of the most picturesque on the island. Bright white posts mark the 'Measured Mile' for ship trials and beside the road are the Corrie quads, four large boulders. The largest, Clach Mhor, is approximately 620 tons. The others are the

◄ *Brodick Castle, Isle of Arran.*

Looking across Brodick Bay to Goat Fell, Isle of Arran. Brodick ▶
Castle is on the far shore, just right of the mast top.

The main thoroughfare, Corrie, Isle of Arran. ▶▶

Elephant Rock (or the Stone of Heroes), the Cat Stone, which gives the best boulder problems for climbers and, further north, the Rocking Stone, which is nearer to Sannox. Force has to be diligently applied to rock this boulder.

Glen Sannox can be either the start or finish of a wonderful walk over the bealach from Glen Rosa and is described at the end of this section. For those not aspiring to such bog-trotting excursions, a walk up the lower reaches of Glen Sannox is still one of the finest in Scotland. Near the start of the glen is a small graveyard dedicated to St Michael and the site of a former monastery. There is also a chambered cairn on the rising ground to the south. However, the old limestone and pyrites workings in the lower glen are still an eyesore.

It is also possible to walk up the coast from North Sannox to the Fallen Rocks, a three-century-old landslide with boulders the size of double-decker buses. There is an alternative path from the A841 a little over a mile out of Sannox from the milestone beyond the North Glen Sannox stream. Beyond the Fallen Rocks is Millstone Point where, as the name implies, millstones were at one time quarried.

Close to the northern point of Arran is the Cock of Arran, so called because at one time it resembled the bird; time and erosion have aged it and so the similarity has disappeared, but it is still a prominent landmark. From the Lodge at Lochranza there is a track to Cock Farm and to Laggan on the coast. There were salt pans in this area and coal was worked in the eighteenth century. From the Cock Farm path you can go round the north-east side of Torr Meadhonach to reach the Cock of Arran. Close by are the Scridain Rocks, a spectacular scree slope—An Scriodan on the map, meaning scree. As with other parts of Arran, this region was evacuated in the 1820s in the Highland Clearances. A fine walk goes down the backbone of this part of the island as far as North Sannox, offering superb views of the main peaks of Arran and over the Firth of Clyde.

Lochranza means the Water of the Rowan Tree. Here is bold scenery with the Glens Easan Biorach and Chalmadale joining forces. The community of Lochranza is small but the castle is an important and a romantic feature. Possibly originally built as a fortified hall house in the thirteenth century, it is mentioned by Fordun as one of the two royal castles of Arran in 1400. As it stands today, it is mostly of sixteenth-century construction, built on an L-plan, with a circular angle-turret at the north-west corner and a machicolated projection on the same level to defend the doorway directly below.

In the vaulted basement is a small prison. Perhaps this was more than adequate, for the castle has had a reasonably tranquil history, its only brush with violence when it was used as a base for James VI's (and I's) sorties against the Clan Donald. It was also used as a base for Cromwell's soldiers later that same century. Now in the care of the Ministry of the Environment, it can be visited seven days a week during the summer months. From Lochranza a summer car ferry operates to the mainland at Claonaig. Burns's Highland Mary was employed in Lochranza by her uncle, the catechist, and her cottage can still be seen.

Gleann Easan Biorach provides a long and generally interesting walk for fourteen miles to Dougarie, midway down the west coast of Arran. It takes one down the central trough of north Arran with the stately peaks of Cir Mhor and Beinn Tarsuinn on the left. A fair section of the route is both trackless and boggy but it ventures into the remote heart of the island. The walk starts at the south-east end of Lochranza village and goes by Loch na Davie and thence over the col or bealach into Glen Iorsa. This glen is then followed down to the sea and the A841.

Going down the west coast of Arran, from Lochranza, Kilbrannan Sound separates the island from Kintyre. This channel was called after St Brandon or Brendan, the famous Celtic missionary who came from Ireland to convert the Picts long before Columba's expedition. St Brandon died in 577 at an advanced age. On the way down this coast

an eye should be kept open for seals and, in the summer months, basking sharks. At Catacol there is a row of houses built about 1850 to house people displaced during the Clearances. These are preserved very much as they were originally (as are those at Corrie). Glen Catacol gives a pleasant walk punctuated by waterfalls. In about two miles a rising line should be taken westwards over the southerly shoulder of Meall nan Damh (510m/1643ft), then downhill into Coire Lochain to the north side of the lochan. Now head a bit north of west to Mid Thundergay.

Further down the main road, heading south, there is a fine example of nineteenth-century dry stone dyking on the left-hand side of the road at Whitefarland.

Southwards, and indeed right round the lower aspect of the island back to Brodick, there is a profusion of standing stones, duns, chambered cairns, stone circles and forts, an archaeologist's paradise. For those with an avid interest the HMSO publication, *Ancient Monuments of Arran* by Robert McLellan, is an essential booklet.

At the south tip of Machrie Bay and a mile from the road is King's Cave. This was claimed to have been Bruce's famous spider cave but it is somewhat unlikely, for his area of operations was on the other side of the island. Easiest access is from the north, from Tormore turn-off where there is a signpost. The rough track should be taken to the last cottage on the shore and from here the path skirts the clifftop for about a mile to dip down into a rocky gulch. The pebbly beach is then followed for a few hundred metres, upon which King's Cave can be located on a higher section of cliffs. The entrance to the cave is protected by a metal grill in which a door is set. It is indeed

◀ *Loch Ranza Castle.*

King's Cave (extreme left), Isle of Arran. This may be the Bruce's ▶
spider cave.

The entrance to King's Cave. ▶▶

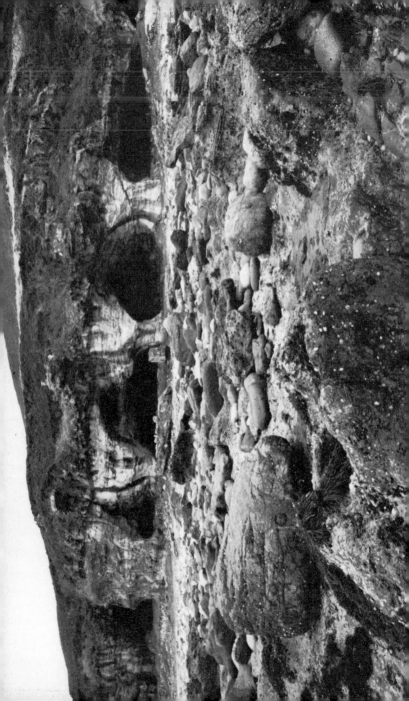

in a fine position and a popular nesting place for a family of fulmars. Inside, it is impressive with rock carvings of hunting scenes, serpents, deer, a floriate cross and a saint. In the past the cross has been mistaken for a claymore. Other legends link the cave with Fionn MacCoul and his legendary Celtic Mafia. One of his sons was reputed to have been born here. As well as the carving of the cross, a stone seat and a small altar have been hewn out of the rock. During the eighteenth century kirk sessions were held in the cave. It is tragic that the spot has been vandalised over the years, but it still retains its majesty.

The standing stones and stone circles of Machrie Moor and Moss Farm are well worth visiting and are only a mile and a half from the road. On Torr Righ Mor, to the east of the road is a huge chambered cairn with a three-apartment chamber. Early Bronze Age relics have been discovered in this area.

On the top of Drumadoon Point there is the site of a twelve-acre Pictish fort known as the Doon. Near here, too, on the cliffs, is Pulpit Rock (aptly named), and close to the golf course yet another stone circle. Drumadoon Farm is the site of Fingal's daughter's grave—a huge trough supported by vertical stones.

Blackwaterfoot is a popular holiday base on the edge of the sandy shores of Drumadoon Bay. Beyond the village, the main road takes a dog's leg inland and from here the String twines northwards. This road was engineered by Telford in 1817 and was the first of the cross-island roads. It rises to 235 metres before angling down to Brodick, with a profusion of good views. String, which also occurs in the String of Lorn, is a corruption of the Gaelic *streng*, meaning bridleway.

Returning to the main coastal road, a mile or so south of Blackwaterfoot at Kilpatrick, is a cashel—a partly fortified, circular settlement of the Celtic Church missionaries from Ireland. These are quite rare in Scotland. Tradition has it that this was the base of St Brandan. The cashel is

The remarkable standing stones of Machrie Moor, Isle of Arran. ▶

located on the inland side of the road to the south of a stream.

At Corriecravie there is the ruin of a fort on Torr a' Chaisteil between the main road and the sea. And a short way further on, beyond the Sliddery Water, the Ross (brother of the String) meets the A841. The Ross follows the Sliddery Water up almost to its watershed at 305 metres, to descend Monamore Glen in a one in six gradient, rejoining the A841 near Lamlash. About two miles up the Ross on the south side, where the road crosses the Sliddery Water, a footpath breaks off north-west, flanking Torr Bhruaich to reach Drimiginar and thence back to the A841. This is a six-mile walk.

Kilmory is a scattering of houses set back about a mile from the shore. Though small, it gives its name to a large parish of some 67,000 acres, incorporating the whole western aspect of the island from Lochranza southwards. On its back door several forest roads and tracks penetrate the conifers of the Forestry Commission, providing pleasant walks which, if the spirit moves one, reach as far as the top end of the Ross. Alternatively there are less strenuous expeditions to Auchdreoch and returning by the road which passes Aucheleffan. Start from the bridge across the Kilmory Water at Kilmory. Close to Aucheleffan a further forest track strikes west and north to reach a stone circle (on the left) about a mile from the junction. The Horned Cairn at Carn Ban is also worth visiting. You must go on foot, however, as cars are not allowed on the road to Auchdreoch. To get to the cairn skirt the farm on the easterly side to reach a gate where a sign indicates the way. The route is marked and takes the shoulder of An Ros, following the line of an old fence. The cairn is located on a slope above a burn. It is trapezoid and the chamber is over five metres wide and about two and a half high, divided into four compartments by three upright slabs.

The 120-metre high cliffs of Bennan Head, the most southerly point of Arran, are only a short distance from East Bennan and there is a chambered cairn on the way.

The Struey Rocks at the head are an interesting feature with their deep-cut fissures in the trap rock. There is also the Black Cave nearby, which is wide and some forty-eight metres long, the largest cave in Arran. It was at one time used for worship and one can't but admire such a setting. For good measure there is also a ruined chapel on the clifftop and a fort close to the Black Cave.

Kildonan, called after St Donnan, who was murdered in 617, is famed for its castle. Bruce has a close association with it and, as mentioned earlier, it was likely that from this castle, in 1307, he spotted the wrong signal from the mainland which triggered off his amazing odyssey. It is a good position on the site of an early Dalriadic fort which utilises one of the natural gullies as part of its defence. The existing structure probably dates from the thirteenth to fourteenth centuries, and comprises three vaulted storeys, though the upper has now collapsed. At basement level the walls are nearly two metres thick. All that remains now is a rickety square tower perched on the clifftop.

Close to the castle is Lloyds Signal Station, weather recording and Coastguard building and just to the west there is a stone circle. A quarter of a mile north-east Port-a-Leacach is a natural causeway of basalt dipping into the sea. The name means Haven of Paved Slabs.

The island of Pladda is hardly half a mile in length and eighteen and a half metres above the high tide mark. It has two lighthouses at the southern end, one which was built by Robert Louis Stevenson's grandfather, Robert Stevenson. On Pladda is the site of St Blaise's Chapel.

Dippin Head, seventy-six metres above the sea, is a splendid viewpoint and above the main road, a short way up the stream, is a chambered cairn. There is a fort below the road at the place where two burns unite in gullies. It is possibly Pictish. Further up the coast, the road takes a northwards swing and on the right, at Largybeg Point, there are standing stones. Largymore is the home of the Giants' Graves (a chambered cairn), now alas much damaged.

From the south end of Whiting Bay it is possible to walk

up from the bowling green in the village to the Forestry road and do the round trip to Kilmory via Auchdreoch, or northwards to Lamlash. Some two miles up this road from South Kiscadale (Whiting Bay), the Glenashdale Burn cuts through a columnar basalt gorge boasting two fine waterfalls, one of these over thirty metres in height. On the left en route to the gorge is the ruin of an early fort.

At the north end of Whiting Bay is Kingscross, where Bruce and his galleys left for the invasion of the Scottish mainland. Here is a Viking grave or ship burial and the site of yet another fort.

Holy Island is spectacular, thrusting truculently out of the sea as if in defiance of loftier tops on Arran. It is sometimes possible to hire a boat from Kingscross Point. Otherwise consult the Tourist Office in Brodick. The island, composed of tiers of columnar clinkstone on sandstone bases, is one and three-quarter miles long and averages about half a mile across—hence its steep appearance, for its high point, Mullach Mor is only 314m/1030ft. The island is dedicated to a certain St Molas who was a bit of a disciplinarian and thought the monastic set-up on Iona too lax, so lived a frugal life in a cave half way along the west shore. It is shallow with a stone shelf bed, a gutter for drip water, a fireplace and 'cupboards' in the rock. Outside is a spring with healing properties, also the Stone of Judgement, with seats carved out of the four corners. There are runic inscriptions referring to Haakon's generals on the cave roof and a signature inscription with an episcopal cross, believed to be that of Nicholas, an eleventh-century Bishop of Man. Ranald, son of Somerled, King of the Isles, was reputed to have founded the monastery at the north-west end of the island, later the site of the island farm. At one time the island was overrun by snakes,

◀ *Kildonan Castle, Isle of Arran. It is possibly from here Bruce saw the signal fire on the Ayrshire coast which started the War of Independence. Ailsa Craig is on the horizon far left; left of the ruin is the lighthouse on Pladda, the original was built by Robert Louis Stevenson's grandfather.*

according to the eighteenth-century traveller, Thomas Pennant. There is a herd of white goats on the east side of the island, descendants of a herd which inhabited Goat Fell until the mid-nineteenth century and gave it its name.

Lamlash gets its name from Eilean Molais, Isle of St Molas, and indeed, looking seaward, Holy Island dominates the skyline. Lamlash is the second most important 'town' on Arran. There is now an annual sea angling festival in the bay where the defeated Haakon licked his wounds and patched his galleys after the Battle of Largs in 1263. In 1548, Mary, Queen of Scots, then five years old, took shelter in the bay en route for France. The island's administrative offices are here. But the Arran Tourist Association Information Office is now at Brodick Pier.

The road between Lamlash and Brodick cuts inland and there is a profusion of stone circles, chambered cairns and standing stones about a mile from the road on the east side. There is also an old fort about a mile north-west of Clauchlands Point which can be reached either from the Brodick end or from Lamlash.

The Arran Hills basically comprise three ridges which run approximately south to north, each divided by well-defined glens. On the easterly side Glen Rosa and Glen Sannox divide Goat Fell from the Beinn Nuis/Cir Mhor ridge, and

Looking up Glen Rosa towards Cir Mhor. The path over the bealach ▶ *to Glen Sannox is to the right of the peak.*

The summit of Cir Mhor can be reached from Fionn Choire, upper ▶ ▶ *Glen Rosa, by taking the easier slopes to the west. The cliffs of Cir Mhor give the best climbing on the island.*

Cir Mhor from the north-west. The easy access slope from Fionn ▶ ▶ *Choire is on the right of the peak. Goat Fell is on the left with the Glen Rosa–Glen Sannox bealach below. The path to the summit of Goat Fell follows the ridge on the left of the photograph.*

these in turn are divided from Beinn Bharrain (721m/2345ft) to the west by Glen Iorsa.

To walk through Glen Rosa to Glen Sannox, start from close to the Auld Kirk in Brodick, leave the String and take the lane to Glen Rosa. The path ends at the farm. The route then takes the west side of the stream with fine views of the granite pyramid of Cir Mhor (798m/2621ft) ahead. To its right is the saddle which must be crossed to gain Glen Sannox. On the left rising above Coire Daingean and Fionn Choire is the granite barrier of the A' Chir ridge. On the right on the slabby westerly side of Goat Fell is the site of the famous Arran murder. (At the trial at the turn of the century John Watson Laurie was convicted of the murder of Edwin Robert Rose by pushing him over a cliff.) The saddle is 430m (1413ft) and once on the other side the path runs for half a mile along the left side of the burn, before crossing to the right-hand side. After passing the old mine, a short walk down the pleasant glen takes you to the main road and from here it is one and a half miles to Corrie. Brodick to Corrie via Glen Rosa and Glen Sannox is eleven miles.

Brodick to Goat Fell via the saddle is for experienced hill walkers. From the saddle you take the shattered ridge on the right to North Goat Fell, and from here bear south to the main summit, avoiding the pinnacles. As well as being the highest point on the island (874m/2866ft), Goat Fell is also one of the finest viewpoints.

The alternative ascent from Brodick is not difficult. Start by the main road at the golf course. Passing the standing stone, take the path on the right which rejoins the road after crossing the stream. Before Brodick Castle, take the road on the left which climbs through the trees. Now follow the path by the Cnocan Burn to Meall Breac, the eastern shoulder of Goat Fell. Keep to the left (west) when the ridge is reached and follow the path to the summit.

The ascent can also be made from the Corrie Burn, just south of Corrie. Follow the forest road to the steeper part of the Corrie Burn and take the path on the true left of the stream (the right as you climb) into the lip of the corrie.

Here the path crosses the stream and climbs south-west on to Meall Breac where it joins up with the path from Brodick.

A satisfactory circuit of Goat Fell and North Goat Fell can be done by taking this track, or the Brodick one, to traverse Goat Fell and North Goat Fell and return by the Corrie Burn. The descent route of North Goat Fell should be to the east which then allows easy access into the corrie of the Corrie Burn. As Arran peaks are frequently cloud covered, having an OS map and a compass is essential, as is being able to use them.

Campbell country: Inveraray to Loch Awe

THIS IS THE heart of the Campbell country where the clan headquarters at Inveraray on Loch Fyne have been established for centuries. Previously they were at Loch Awe but moved after achieving their supremacy over the MacDonalds. The Lordship of the Isles, the greatest in Scottish history, crumbled owing to its participation in rebellions which caused the forfeiture of the MacDonald lands in 1493. The Campbells, who had supported Robert the Bruce against Edward I of England, stepped into MacDonald shoes and became an all-powerful and much hated clan.

A castle was first built close to the present site way back in 1415 by one Colin Campbell of Loch Awe, but by 1743 the third duke felt that it needed mod-cons and decided to rebuild both castle and nearby village which was also, he thought, in need of a facelift. In any case, the village was a bit too close for privacy. Duly, the town was rebuilt half a mile south at Gallows Foreland. The programme was not completed until 1794, however, by the fifth duke.

Both town and castle are well worth visiting and castle and grounds are open to the public.

A pleasant walk can be done from the road-end (or rather from the stile by the locked gate) in upper Glen Shira to Rob Roy's Cottage. This notorious bandit, Rob

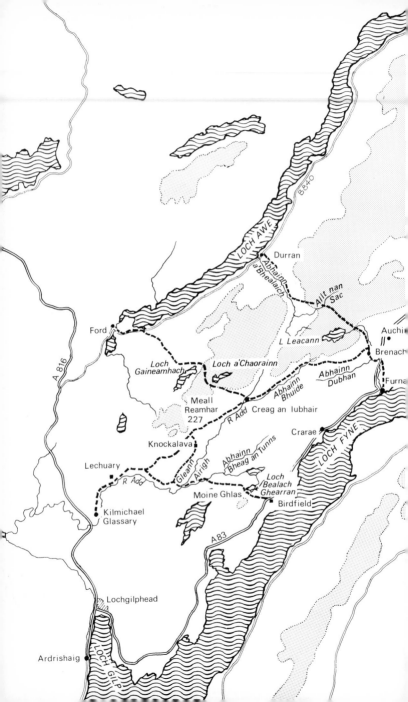

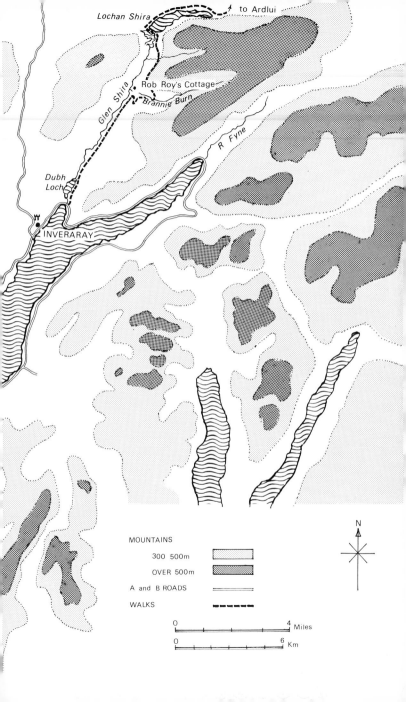

Lochan Shira

to Ardlui

Glen Shira

Rob Roy's Cottage

Brannie Burn

R Fyne

Dubh
Loch

INVERARAY

MOUNTAINS

300 500m

OVER 500m

A and B ROADS

WALKS

0   4 Miles

0   6 Km

N

Roy MacGregor, who was given refuge by the Campbells, lived for eight years in Glen Shira. You can walk up either side of the glen and reach the cottage by the true left bank of the river (that is the right-hand bank going up). From the locked gate, walk several miles up the glen to where a deer fence is reached on the left, just before a bend in the road. Now cut down towards the left and pass through a gate in the deer fence where an ill-defined path leads to a bridge over the Brannie Burn. Beyond this you come to a ruin, which is not Rob Roy's Cottage. This lies about two hundred metres beyond, just above the Shira River in a clearing made by the Forestry Commission. Little is left but the ruined walls.

Past the turn-off to Rob Roy's Cottage there is a long walk (twenty-two miles from Inverary) through to Ardlui on Loch Lomond. Take the forest track to Lochan Shira dam. Then, by skirting the northern shore of the lochan in an easterly direction, reach the shallow pass, and the Allt an Taillir. Follow the stream to where it turns south, then continue east to meet with a track descending the Dubh Eas to Glen Falloch, and the main road two and a half miles north of Ardlui.

Five miles south of Inveraray on the A83 is Auchindrain where an attempt had been made to restore old houses with the support of the National Museum of Antiquities and two Scottish universities. Just a mile beyond the village, at Leacann Water, is where the last wolf in mid-Argyll was slaughtered two centuries ago—by a woman wielding a spindle. The woman didn't survive the encounter, for her body was found alongside the dead wolf. She had died of shock!

The A83 returns to Loch Fyne at Furnace from where there are two excellent walks to Loch Awe. The first, to Durran, is some six and a half miles and starts one and

---

▲ *Inveraray Castle, seat of the Argyll Campbells.*

◀ *Inveraray from the harbour.*

a half miles to the north of the village. Follow the road along the Abhainn Dubhan, then strike north-west past Brenachoille to take the path up the west bank of the Leacann Water. Pass on the north side of Loch Leacann and now go north-west on the moorland and, about a mile and a half after crossing the Allt nan Sac, go down gently to Abhainn a' Bhealaich. Follow this glen to Durran.

The other route goes from Furnace to Ford at the foot of Loch Awe and was obviously an old clan or coffin road; the distance is about sixteen miles. At the Loch Awe end, just a few hundred metres above the loch is the ruin of a St Columba church (described in detail in *A circuit of Loch Awe*). The walk starts as for the Furnace–Durran route as far as Brenachoille, then takes the track following the Abhainn Bhuidhe to Creag-an-Iubhair. Follow the track westwards now to the south side of Loch a' Chaorainn and pass the north side of Loch Gaineamhach. Now go north-west to Loch Awe about one and a half miles from Ford. A diversion can be made on this route from Creag-an-Iubhair by continuing down the Gleann Airigh via Meall Reamhar (227m/744ft) to the River Add at Lechuary. From here it is two and a half miles south to Kilmichael Glassary. The distance is also sixteen miles.

Crarae is three miles south of Furnace and here the gardens are well worth a visit, being among the best in Argyllshire. Thirty-three acres were developed by Sir George I. Campbell of Succoth who enlarged upon the existing garden. The exotic collection of rhododendrons, conifers and azaleas, and a profusion of other trees and shrubs are now under the care of the research branch of the Forestry Commission and is open all year. The gardens are in a wild setting and a day crammed with exercise and interest can be had in their exploration.

Continuing down Loch Fyne-side to Birdfield, a forest road cuts inland which offers a forest route to join up with the Furnace–Kilmichael Glassary walk mentioned earlier. Take the forest road past Loch Bealach Ghearran and

◄ *All that's left of Rob Roy's cottage, Glen Shira.*

the Moine Ghlas to cross the Abhainn Bheag an Tunns. Now the road runs more or less parallel with this until it crosses the River Add, where it turns to the north to meet up with the Furnace–Kilmichael Glassary route beyond Knockalava. The distance is in the region of five and a half miles to the junction of the routes. However, instead of cutting all the way back to the Furnace–Kilmichael Glassary track (unless you wish to head back to Furnace) take the first left track after crossing the River Add and gain the Furnace–Kilmichael Glassary track in approximately one and a half miles. The distance is about ten miles.

Crinan Canal is a gateway to the Atlantic for yachtspeople wishing to avoid the vagaries of weather off the Mull of Kintyre. The canal was cut in 1801 by Thomas Telford and in nine miles it links the Sound of Jura with the Loch Gilp arm of Loch Fyne, saving an eighty mile voyage round the Mull of Kintyre. In the terminal basins you can often see 'puffers', the small gruff terrier-like cargo boats immortalised by Neil Munro's *Vital Spark*, now used for holidays afloat. Brushing shoulders with these are slick yachts and no-nonsense fishing boats. However, we will return to Crinan when we complete the circuit of the Kintyre peninsula.

South of Lochgilphead and Ardrishaig the A83 still hugs the shore of Loch Fyne as if scared to enter the hinterland of Knapdale, the region lying to the south of the Crinan Canal. Knapdale is separated from Kintyre by the neck of land between East and West Loch Tarbert, which applies a tourniquet to Kintyre. Knapdale means hill and dale, and this is apt, but its easterly side has little to offer before Tarbert. A loop road, the B8024, encircles South Knapdale (with the help of the A83) and this gives access to otherwise remote country. We will return to explore Knapdale once we have completed our tour round Kintyre.

A puffer taking its ease at Crinan on the western end of the Crinan Canal. ▶

Tarbert is a picturesque fishing village, with houses crowding the bay as if eager to see the catches of the fishing boats. Though the village is small it is important, for it serves as an almost perfect anchorage for boats heading up to Ardrishaig and Crinan, and across the narrow isthmus at West Loch Tarbert is the terminus for the Islay and Jura ferries.

The busy south pier is where landings of the famous Loch Fyne herrings are made, alas now in restricted catches. Large, oily, plump and known locally as 'Glasgow Magistrates', they have a delicious flavour, both fresh or when oak-chip kippered.

It is worth clambering up to the crumbled ruin of Tarbert Castle above the south pier. Now little remains but the decaying fifteenth-century keep. At one time the castle was large and dates from an early age. Selbach, King of Lorne, burnt it in 712. Robert the Bruce added a courtyard seventy-three metres by ninety and made some repairs. He

also built a house and hall inside the older part. The bills for all this work are still on record in the old Exchequer Rolls. It cost £511. Tarbert (or Tarbet) means a place where boats can be ferried overland, and when Bruce occupied Tarbert Castle he had his galley taken across the isthmus on rollers—wind assisted, according to John Barbour's *Bruce*:

> ". . . and since the wind blew strong behind them [as] they went, he [Bruce] had ropes and masts set up in the ships and sails fastened to the tops, and caused the men to go drawing alongside. The wind that was blowing helped them, so that in a little space the whole fleet was safely drawn across."

Two centuries before Bruce the same crossing was made by the long ships of the twenty-year-old Norse King Magnus Barefoot. He was about to launch a surprise attack on the Scottish mainland against Malcolm III, King of Scots. Malcolm's father had been killed by Macbeth in 1040, but Malcolm killed Macbeth in battle in 1057. Malcolm was fed-up with the Norse harassment and agreed that Norway should retain the Hebrides and that the Vikings have the land round which a boat could sail. So whilst Magnus sat at the tiller, his boat was 'sailed' overland between East and West Loch Tarbert. In the late 1700s, before the Crinan Canal was excavated by the industrious Telford, boats of nine to ten tons were dragged by horses across this isthmus.

To the Mull of Kintyre

THOUGH THE WEST coast road down Kintyre is the better, the road on the east coast is the most scenic and has a peculiar charm. Skipness is reached by a branch road

▲ *Fishing boats in Tarbert Harbour.*

◀ *Looking across East Loch Tarbert towards Tarbert Castle, once held by Robert the Bruce.*

running back up the coast for a couple of miles from the B842, for the coastline immediately south of Tarbert is roadless and it is only at Claonaig that Loch Fyne-side is reached again.

Skipness in Norse means Ship Point. There was once a steamer service to Skipness, but storms swept away the old pier. The old castle of square Norman design is situated, strangely for these parts, on flat terrain. The original tower (now the north-west corner) was built in 1220 when Donald of Islay was King of the Isles and Kintyre. The castle is built in the form of a rectangle, twenty-seven metres by forty, and the reason for its good preservation is because it never had to withstand a major siege. It seems unusually endowed with garderobes (free-fall loos)! To the south-east of the castle, several hundred metres across the machair, stand the ruins of Kilbrannan Chapel amidst its burial ground, another dedication to St Brandon. The existing building dates from the thirteenth or fourteenth century. On the floor are various grave-slabs, one depicting lady and knight, deer and hounds. There are also several fine stones outside. It is pleasant to wander by the point and look at the eider duck, or to take the old road from Skipness Burn, by the castle car park, two and a half miles north-east over the open moorland.

The next place which takes one's fancy going down the coast is Carradale. The harbour, built in 1959, is as picturesque as any Cornish cove. The pier is usually chock-a-block with fishing boats, and when the crew are not unloading their catches, they wield paintbrushes, giving their sturdy crafts a facelift.

The beach at Carradale Bay is a superb expanse of sand, flanked on the east by a rocky tidal promontory which seems to hang onto the mainland at low tide. To reach the beach, take the road to Port Righ and where this turns

Skipness Castle. The basic tower, now the north-west corner, was ▶
built around 1220 by Donald of Islay, King of the Isles and Kintyre.

The war memorial clock at St Brandon's church, Skipness. ▶▶

abruptly left, a gate and rough track directly ahead give access to a beach three-quarters of a mile long, backed by whin, rhododendrons and machair, the strip grazing adjoining many west-coast beaches.

The area is now a nature reserve, administered by the Scottish Wildlife Trust. Seals sport on the rocks of the point, and dolphins and even whales are occasionally spotted in the summer. A herd of wild white goats may be seen browsing on the scant fare of rocky ledges. There are also many eider duck which, with their learner ducklings in tow, provide an engaging scene as they jostle in the waves.

On the tidal point there is a vitrified Iron Age fort which is well worth visiting. It is an exhilarating short walk, picking through rocky outcrops studded with flowers in the spring. The large circular fort, or what is left of it after several thousand years, is nearly forty metres in diameter, and the best vitrified fort in Argyllshire.

The village of Saddell lies in the arms of its wood where time and indeed most of the traffic seem to pass it by; yet here, in 1158, the body of Somerled was, by repute, laid to rest. He was the only Scot and King of the Isles to defeat the Vikings on their own element—the sea. Perhaps being half-Norse himself helped. On the south side of the river his son Reginald, King of the Isles, completed a Cistercian monastery begun by and dedicated to his father. Not much remains of the original cruciform-shaped building, nine metres wide by over forty long. It is said that one of the old recumbent tombstones with Celtic carvings in the graveyard is that of Somerled. Also here his descendant, Angus Og, Lord of the Isles, is said to have welcomed Robert the Bruce in 1306 when he landed at Ugadale. The collection of medieval sword-slabs is very fine, now under cover close to the entrance. In the north transept, one of the knights portrayed is said to represent Somerled.

Half a mile south-east of the abbey, close to the shore, stands Saddell Castle. It was built in 1508 by one David

◀ *Carradale harbour, Kintyre.*

Hamilton, Bishop of Argyll. It's an oblong keep fifteen and a half metres high, with machicolated parapets. Above the entrance is the Clan Donald coat of arms: the galley of Somerled, symbol of sea power. The castle has been restored.

Before one reaches Campbeltown, there is a walk which strikes inland through the Saddell Forest from Kildonan and after crossing Glenlussa Water takes the left-hand track back south at the T-junction just below the toe of Lussa Loch, to reach the A83 near Drumore. It is approximately nine miles.

Looking at the map, Campbeltown has the appearance of having been exiled on the end of its long peninsula for some nefarious deed long ago. Yet, it is well served by both air and sea, being only forty minutes' flying time from Glasgow to Machrihanish airport on the west coast. The town isn't exactly pleasing to the eye, but on the other hand it's not too vulgar either, and both the esplanade and the harbour do it justice. Immediately behind the old quay is Campbeltown Cross, a carved fifteenth-century Celtic wheel cross of dignified aloofness. Its history is unknown. It stands on a seven-step plinth and has a Latin inscription: "This is the cross of Master Ivar Maceachern, Rector of Kilregan and Andrew his son, Rector of Kilcoman who erected the cross"—an interesting comment on clerical celibacy, if nothing more. It is customary for local funerals to pass the cross and here, too, the New Year is brought in.

At one time Campbeltown was famous for its distilleries; in 1880 there were twenty, now alas only two.

Davaar Island, close to Campbeltown, acts as a mercy breakwater to the harbour. It is no longer inhabited, but its northerly point still boasts of a lighthouse, built in 1784. The approach to the island is via the Kilkerran road from Campbeltown about a couple of miles from the Old Quay. It can be reached at low tide by a connecting shingle

◀ *The best surviving Iron Age vitrified fort in Argyll, on a tidal islet in Carradale Bay. Inset is detail of the composition of the vitrified walls.*

bank called the Dhorlin. On the south coast of the island are several caves. The wall of one, lit by a convenient aperture in the rock, shows a life-size painting of the Crucifixion, created in secret by thirty-three-year-old Alexander MacKinnon in 1887, as an act of piety after a shipwreck; at the age of eighty he returned to retouch his masterpiece. There are seven caves in the southern cliffs and the painting cave is the fifth as you come from the Dhorlin.

At the New Quay in Campbeltown the self-righting lifeboat lies at the ready on her moorings, a combination of technology and tradition, merged into a life-saving machine. The history of the Campbeltown lifeboat is as long as Kintyre itself, and many sagas have been enacted round the 300-metre storm-hounded cliffs of the Mull.

A fascinating collection of gravestones from the site of old Saddell Abbey near Carradale. ▶

▼ *Campbeltown's self-righting lifeboat.*

SADDELL ABBEY STONES

THE STONES BROUGHT HERE FROM
SADDELL ABBEY FOR PRESERVATION
WERE ALL CARVED IN ARGYLL IN
THE PERIOD 1300–1500.
OF PARTICULAR INTEREST ARE THE
THREE EFFIGIES OF MEN WEARING
THE TYPE OF ARMOUR THAT WAS
IN VOGUE IN THE LOCALITY IN THE
14TH AND 15TH CENTURIES, AND EFFIGY
OF A PRIEST IDENTIFIED BY HIS
VESTMENTS AND BY THE PRESENCE
OF A CHALICE. THE FIGURE
(NOW HEADLESS) OF ONE OF THE
CISTERCIAN MONKS OF THE ABBEY,
AND FRAGMENTS OF A CROSS.
OF THE FLAT GRAVE-SLABS INCLUDES
OF THE ELABORATE DECORATION
FOLIAGE-SCROLLS, SWORDS, WEST
HIGHLAND GALLEYS, DEER-HUNTS,
CASKETS AND SHEARS

Now their missions are shared with the Navy Sea King helicopters based at Prestwick.

Southend Kintyre is close to the tip of the peninsula, with the blue Antrim hills a mere seventeen miles away but looking much closer. One of the principal landmarks is Dunaverty Rock, where once stood an imposing and strategic castle of the Lord of the Isles, built on the site of an ancient dun during the thirteenth century. Virtually nothing remains, but standing there one can imagine its importance at this maritime crossroads. Angus II, the fifth Lord of the Isles, was host here to Bruce in 1306 and one of his chief supporters during the War of Independence. When the English fleet arrived, Angus spirited him across the channel to Ireland. Though the English laid siege to the castle, this was repulsed.

A couple of hundred years after Bruce's bed and hurried breakfast, King James IV was at Tarbert repairing the castle when he impetuously decided to sail to the Southend and seize Dunaverty—which he did. The King left a garrison at Dunaverty and took his leave, well satisfied with his work. However, Sir John of Islay, who owned castle and land, and who had considered the King a friend, bitterly resented the action. So before the King's ship rounded nearby MacShannon's Point, Sir John retook the castle and, in view of the King, hanged the Governor from the curtain walls.

In 1607 the castle, and indeed the whole of Kintyre, became the property of the Campbells, and in 1647, during the wars of Montrose, the castle was taken by Sir Alexander MacDonald. When General Leslie and his Covenanter force closed in, Sir Alexander withdrew to Ireland, leaving a garrison of 300 good men. After a long siege, the garrison surrendered for lack of water and in one of the most savage incidents in this bloody holy war, upon the instigation of a minister, John Neave, all 300 men were massacred and the castle razed to the ground.

Dunaverty Bay is indeed fine, but an even better beach

◄ *The fifteenth-century Campbeltown Cross beside the Old Quay.*

is at Macharioch, some three miles east, with views to the Ayrshire coast and the Ailsa Craig.

On the west shore of Dunaverty Bay is Keil, and beyond the hotel on a shoulder of the hill, the thirteenth-century chapel. It contains some interesting medieval sword-stones and an effigy slab. At the west end of the burial ground on a small knoll are the imprints on the rock of two feet, one pointing east, the other north. By repute, they are supposed to have been the 'footprints' of St Columba, who is said to have landed here when he first came over from Ireland. (Perhaps early observers failed to see that, as well as being splay-footed, St Columba appeared to have had two right feet.) Columba's coracle couldn't have been a very good sea boat, so it does seem logical that he would have made as short a sea journey as possible. However, the print carvings are not contemporaneous. The east–west one is about 3,000 years old, the other is believed to have been re-cut in 1856 by a local called McIlrevie (witnessed by his grandson), and is possibly Columba's print, indicating the direction of his mission. Cut alongside is the date 546, which is obviously fake. It is possible that, as at Dunadd to the north, the older print may have had a pagan symbolism and it is known that Columba utilised such ready-made holiness; even his Iona base was on an old Druid site.

Some two hundred metres west of the hillock are three caves at the base of a sandstone cliff. The larger cave was probably occupied from the third century and in the small one to its eastern side is a cup-marked stone which may have been a Druid altar.

Just west of Keil a road runs up Glen Breackerie. From the head of the glen a track leads to the sea. There are caves festooned with stalactites at Uamh Ropa. If time permits it is also worth climbing Cnoc Moy (446m/1462ft) for the superb view.

A trip to the Mull lighthouse is most rewarding, either on a good day or a stormy one, when the wild home waters of the Campbeltown lifeboat can be well appreciated. This is rough country and one must take to shank's pony at a pass called the Gap (350m/1150ft). Here cars must be abandoned and the way down the steep zig-zags made on foot, for descent on wheels is prohibited. It's one mile, and a drop of 259m/850ft to the lighthouse. Due to its elevated position, the lighthouse is a sawn-off job, open to the public at the discretion of the keeper. From here houses and trees on the coast of Ireland, a mere twelve miles off, can be seen distinctly, as well as the nearer Rathlin Island lighthouse.

The beach at Machrihanish is the longest in Argyll, the bottom end of which curves westwards, forming Machrihanish Bay. Here, as mentioned, is Campbeltown's airport and an elegant golf course on the springy machair. The best part of the beach is to the north, nearer Westport, where creeks open on to dazzling sand, giving shelter from the wind.

At Westport one is on the commuting route of the A83, the main road linking the Mull of Kintyre to the north. Though it is often dismissed as uninteresting compared with the more scenic eastern road it offers fine views westwards and indeed there are some pleasant walks to be savoured. One starts a mile north of Westport at Tangy Lodge and runs north to Bellochantuy, about three miles, with two or three ruined duns by the way.

Gigha is a sun-blessed island lying off the west coast of Kintyre. The name means God Island or Good Island and is pronounced Gee-a. It is most readily reached by ferryboat from Tayinloan. The three-mile crossing takes about half an hour.

For anyone with botanical leanings Gigha is a must, for Sir James Horlick's garden at Achamore House is one of the finest in Scotland, ranking with Colonsay and Inverewe. Sir James donated the plant collection to the National Trust for Scotland and the gardens are open to the public daily from dawn to dusk, April to September inclusive.

Sir James should really be the patron saint of Gigha, for he has done much good for the island and its inhabitants; not only did he create the gardens, but helped in the establishment of dairy herds and the widely renowned Gigha cheese.

The island is long and narrow, six miles by one and a half on average. In a small chapel dedicated to St Cattan there are several medieval grave-slabs. The chapel is south of Ardminish, half a mile past the hotel. Just west, on top of a knoll, is a slender standing stone inscribed with Ogham characters now, alas, barely discernible.

At Leim in the south-west of the island is a subterranean passage about forty metres long. At high water the tide runs through this and during storms water spouts erupt through two apertures.

Gigha's many bays, skerries and dales make it an altogether delightful place, well worth a visit.

Islay: Barnacle Geese and distilleries

ISLAY IS AN island of farming and whisky distilling, tourism taking very much a back seat in the island's economy. There is an atmosphere of self-sufficiency here, where the B & B sign seems an endangered species. You can get to Islay by car ferry and steamer from West Loch Tarbert to Port Ellen, or by air from Glasgow.

The anvil-like peninsula of Kilchoman looks as if it was added onto the rest of the island as an afterthought. Indeed, it was a separate island at one time. Port Charlotte (where the street names are in Gaelic) is the principal centre of habitation on this part of the island, with the Rinns of Islay as its back garden. There really are walks everywhere; all you have to do is grab your map and your mac and head off. For example, going out of town by the road to Kilchiaran, a footpath cuts off left just before Cnoc na Buaile to meet up with the Portnahaven road. Go right here and follow the road to Kilchiaran where the roofless St Chiaran Chapel is worth inspection, with a cup-marked stone lying between the gate and the church. These rock indentations, varying in diameter from twenty-six to seventy-five millimetres, and decorated round the edges with carved rings or spirals, are often to be found on Bronze Age cists or passage graves. There are other interesting features, including a stone altar and various cross-slabs.

From Kilchiaran a track going north takes you to Machir Bay. You can also drive close to the bay from the A847 to Kilchoman. To the west there is nothing until you reach America and life appears to have a siesta quality about it. There is an inshore lifeboat here as well as a Coastguard Station, and though the gaunt-looking church is not a structure to raise the spirits, the graveyard has some very fine stones and crosses. A two and a half metre high cross was erected here by John, Lord of the Isles, in the fourteenth century in memory of his second wife, Princess Margaret, daughter of Robert II. There is an interesting artifact for expectant mothers at the base of the cross, a round wishing stone on a stone basin. All a mother-to-be has to do is to turn the stone to guarantee a son.

About a quarter of a mile to the south-west is a cemetery maintained by the War Graves Commission, which includes some seventy-four stones in memory of the captain and crew of HMS *Otranto*, torpedoed off this savage coast in October 1918—a month before the end of the war. A short way east from here is a listing wheel cross of unknown date.

On Loch Gorm, a couple of miles to the north, is an island where the MacDonalds had a castle. They also had a summer residence on the shore. The loch and all the way to Ardnave Point is a favourite wintering spot for wild geese. A quarter of the world population of Barnacle Geese uses Islay.

Before the end of the road leading towards Ardnave Point are the remains of Cill Naoimh between the road and the shore of Loch Gruinart. This now roofless chapel has violent memories. There was a battle, MacDonalds versus MacLeans, at the head of the loch in 1598. The MacDonalds won on points and pursued the thirty MacLeans to the sanctuary of the chapel. Enraged because they thought their young chief, Sir James of Dunivaig, had been killed—in fact he only had an arrow in his

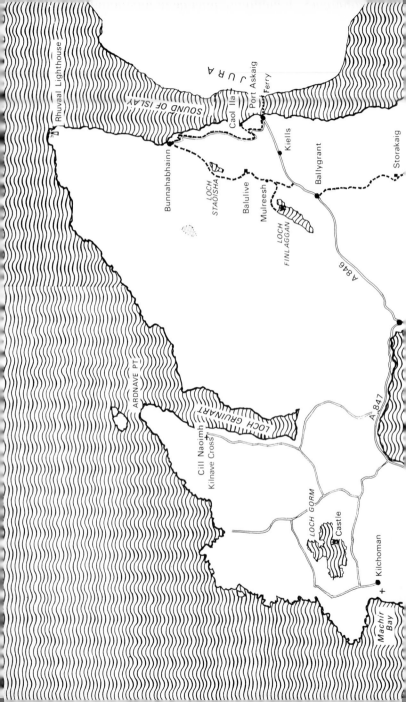

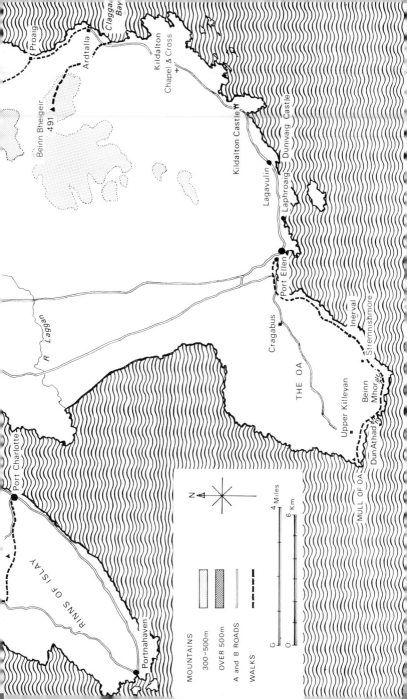

MOUNTAINS

300–500m

OVER 500m

A and B ROADS

WALKS

N

4 Miles

6 Km

Proaig

Claggan Bay

Ardtalla

Kildalton

Chapel & Cross

Beinn Bheigeir ▲ 491

Kildalton Castle

Lagavulin

Laphroaig

Dunyvaig Castle

R. Laggan

Port Ellen

Cragabus

Inerval

Stremnishmore

THE OA

Upper Killeyan

Beinn Mhor

MULL OF OA

Dun Athad

Port Charlotte

RINNS OF ISLAY

Portnahaven

leg—they barred the MacLeans inside the chapel (you can still see the bar-holes in the entrance) and burned them alive. In the adjoining churchyard stands the Kilnave High Cross, large-armed, but not quite symmetrical.

To the east of Loch Gruinart is a tract of wild and roadless country, a land of lochs, rocks and hills, with a storm-battered coastline running to Rhuvaal Lighthouse at the northern tip of Islay. The lighthouse, built in 1859, presents a red light to the west and white on all other bearings.

At first, the east coast of Islay runs north–south from the lighthouse till it enters the confines of the Sound of Islay and here, remarkably, is the community and distillery of Bunnahabhainn, a self-contained industrial centre. From the sea, the sight of this place for alcoholic sailors must be like an oasis. And if the same sailors continue south down the narrowing Sound of Islay, they will have a double-take when they see Caol Ila Distillery, cowering under a cliff with its own jetty, like a deep-water refuelling base. Both these places can be reached by a road which runs north from the A846 just outside Port Askaig. Alternatively, a more varied walk begins from the side road to Mulreesh, about two and a half miles out of Port Askaig on the A846. Before you come to Mulreesh a farm road on the left, going to Finlaggan Farm, can be used to reach Loch Finlaggan. On an island in this loch is a medieval keep and curtain walls with round towers, all that remains of a castle of the Lords of the Isles, where in ages past the Kings of Man and the Lords of the Isles were proclaimed. There was a chapel on the island at one time and many sculptured slabs survive. A nearby islet was used as a meeting place for the Lord's council, and another as a prison. From the Mulreesh road-end beyond Balulive you can follow a track just over two miles to Bunnahabhainn, round the top of Loch Staoisha.

Port Askaig sits on the shore at the narrow part of the Sound of Islay. It is a pleasant place, base for the Islay

Port Askaig, Islay. On the left is the Islay lifeboat.   ▶

lifeboat and the Jura car ferry, and calling point for Caledonian MacBrayne steamers. With the shipping terminal, the hotel and the post office, there's not much room for anything else. The main centre of population is a mile away, up the steep hill at Keills.

Going inland, the next place of consequence is Bowmore. This village of some 600 souls is at the hub of Islay. The unusual circular parish church of Killarrow commands attention from its hill overlooking the town, contemplating wrongdoers. These Islay distilleries are like pub doors at present, constantly closing, then opening again. South of Bowmore lies a wide area of peat, even today a main source of fuel for the islanders and for malting barley for the distilleries. Running across this are two roads, a short distance apart. The High Road, the B8016, was started in 1841 to provide employment during the great potato famine. The A846 was started in 1885, and has the airport on its western flank.

Port Ellen is the second largest community on Islay, but it is no showpiece, though the setting is fine. The town is crowded to the side of the encircling arm of a south-facing bay. However, the great nosebags of the distillery, the grain silos, don't enhance the landscape. There are regular sailings from here to West Loch Tarbert.

Following the A846 east of Port Ellen you pass the Laphroaig Distillery, and yet another at Lagavoulin. Here, guarding the small bay (and seemingly the distillery) is the run-down Dunivaig Castle. This at one time was a principal stronghold of the Lords of the Isles and stands on the site of an early dun. It has a long and chequered history. In an attempt to subdue the unruly clansmen James VI gave orders to Huntly to exterminate the islanders. Fortunately, Huntly never got to Islay, but the Campbells did; they took the castle using cannon in 1615. It was also besieged in 1646.

The circular parish church of Killarrow, Islay, said to be an eighteenth-century copy of an ancient church in Jerusalem. ▶

Further along the road on the right, hidden in the trees, is the ruin of Kildalton Castle. One wonders if the gate-house has white mice to match its fairytale exterior, for it was built of white quartzite in the Scottish baronial style in the nineteenth century. Three miles beyond, on the right, is a side road going to the old Kildalton church and grave-yard. This is the home of the famed Kildalton High Cross, probably the finest in all Scotland. It is carved from a single piece of Epiorite, local stone of a greenish hue, and probably executed by an Iona stonemason. There are many other stones of interest in this fascinating graveyard. If you go to Islay, this place is a must; it is worth going to Islay just to see the cross.

For hill walkers there are two walks at the end of this road which follows the coast to Ardtalla, just north of Claggain Bay. A path continues up the coast to Proaig, then goes north-west across a lonely stretch to Storakaig. From here take the track and road to reach the A846 at Ballygrant. The distance is about ten miles.

The hill walk up Beinn Bheigeir takes one at 491m (1609ft) to the highest point on Islay. From the north end of Claggain Bay, head for the hill and take a line to the high point on the skyline. Thereafter, follow its broad back to the north-west end, which is the summit.

The Oa (pronounced 'oh') is a super part of Islay, if you don't mind being windblown and enjoy heady cliffs and acres of sea. The Oa is a spit of land that juts out into the Atlantic to the west of Port Ellen. You can walk to it from that ninety-per-cent-proof-smelling town by taking a path from the cemetery at the west side of the bay and following it round the coast to Inerval. Take the farm road on from there to Stremnishmore, where it ends. You then contour round the hillside to the cairn at Beinn Mhor (202m/656ft) near the cliff edge, and continue past Dun Athad on the next point. An eye should be kept out for the wild goats which operate on these cliffs. (One wonders if there aren't

◀ *The Kildalton High Cross, Islay, one of the finest in all Scotland.*

easier ways of getting a bite.) The clifftop now takes you round to the great American monument close to the Mull of Oa which commemorates US troops drowned in torpedoed ships in 1918.

It is also possible to reach the monument by taking the Cragabus road from just north-west of Port Ellen and following it to near Upper Killeyan Farm. The path from here is signposted. The coastline of the Oa is wild and savage and the granite cliffs and ridges below Beinn Mhor are popular with rock climbers, giving routes of over sixty metres.

The 'horrid ile' of Jura

COMPARED WITH NEIGHBOURING Islay, Jura is a wild place. Way back in 1646, Sir James Turner wrote of it: "Jura, a horrid ile and a habitation fit for deers and wild beasts." The name Jura means Deer Island in the Norse or, to those with a more cynical disposition, it can also be interpreted as 'dull' or 'dour'.

There is one way to get to Jura (unless you have your own boat). That is from Port Askaig on Islay, where the car ferry plies to Feolin. From Feolin, where there is nothing but a draught and a fine view across to Islay, the car-width road doubles round the bottom end of the island to stay on the east coast until it runs out way up in the north end.

Craighouse is Jura's main centre of population and, as one would expect with so many thirsty people on the mainland, a distillery town with a hotel and not a great deal else. About a mile up the road is the small crofting community of Keils. All Keils have their chapels from 'cille', which means chapel, and this is no exception, but is more interesting than most. It was dedicated to an Iona

◄ *The American monument on the Mull of Oa, commemorating US troops torpedoed in 1918.*

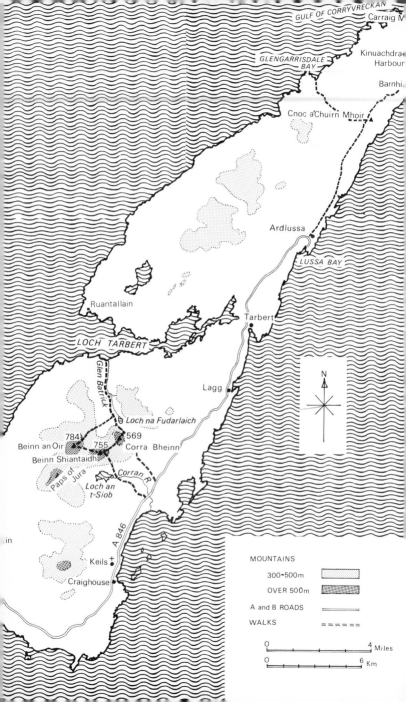

missionary called St Earnadail. Though he lived (and died) on Islay, he left instructions that he should be buried here, stating that the exact spot where he was to be laid to rest would be indicated by a ball of mist; a not too infrequent phenomenon in these parts, one must acknowledge. This graveyard is also the terminal home of the Campbells of Jura and of one Gillouir MacCrain, whose headstone claims that he died at the grand old age of 180 years. (Longevity ran in the family, for his daughter Mary lies just up the coast at Inverlussa, though she was careless enough to burn herself out in 1856 at the comparatively early age of 128.) Keils chapel and graveyard occupy a delightful spot, with a dancing stream half a mile to the north. The stream is known as the Minister's Burn and the manse is nearby.

The twenty-four mile long Jura road provides some superb views coastwards and also inland at times to the high hills of the island, the Paps of Jura. Not two, as students of anatomy might expect, but many, adorning the lower half of the island.

Beinn Shiantaidh (755m/2477ft) is the second highest peak on Jura, and as well as being a very fine viewpoint, is reasonably easy of access. You leave the road at the Corran River on the true right bank (that is the left looking up), and cut up to the higher ground to the right of the plantation. Contour round to Loch an t-Siob, keeping to the drier ground, then go across the river where it leaves the loch. Now, with resolution, tackle the mixed quartzite scree slopes above until the summit is reached, unless poor visibility or weather dictates retreat. If the flesh is willing, it is now possible to move on to another pap, Beinn an Oir (784m/2571ft) by descending to the col between Beinn Shiantaidh and Beinn an Oir. There is a causeway rising to the summit of Beinn an Oir. This was constructed in 1812 by the Ordnance Survey when experiments were made to determine the boiling temperature of water at various altitudes. Descend to the north-east to reach the Glen Batrick path near Loch na Fudarlaich. As this excursion is reasonably energetic, make sure you are fit enough to

MARY MACCRAIN
DIED IN 1856, AGED 128
DESCENDANT OF
GILLOUR MACCRAIN
WHO KEPT
A HUNDRED & EIGHTY CHRISTMASSES
IN HIS OWN HOUSE
AND WHO DIED IN THE
REIGN OF CHARLES I

complete it and, as with other hill walks, that you take a map and compass.

As an alternative, it is feasible to take in the summit of Corra Bheinn (569m/1863ft) after Beinn Shiantaidh. From the summit of Beinn Shiantaidh the descent is steep as is the climb. It adds some three and a half miles and an extra 203 metres. Corra Bheinn can also be climbed from the Glen Batrick track. One end of this path starts just under a mile beyond the road bridge over the Corran River. It is a walk of about five and a half damp and lonely miles across the island, but the western coastline at Glenbatrick is worth the hike, with its caves and natural arches and spectacularly raised beaches illustrating how the sea has dropped some fifteen metres.

The island is almost cut in two at Loch Tarbert, another of those busy places where ships used to be dragged overland. At Lagg, just before these land narrows, a ferry once operated to Keills in Knapdale, where cattle were unloaded on to the superb dry stone jetty en route for the trysts, or markets, on the mainland. There is nothing much at Tarbert itself, a chapel site and burial ground, and a few standing stones looking bored, the big one two and a half metres tall.

At Ardlussa the metalled road stops. It is still possible to drive on for a way, though it does get outbackish after a while. In any case, it is pleasant walking and after nine miles the road ends just beyond Kinuachdrach Harbour.

There is a further two miles to go before you reach Carraig Mhor and there you run out of Jura. Ahead is the Gulf of Corryvreckan with its famous whirlpool, the world's second largest. This awesome Hag is best viewed from the island of Scarba on the other side of the gulf and access is described in the last section of the book, *Oban to Crinan*.

It is of interest to note that George Orwell stayed for several years at the remote and lovely house of Barnhill,

◀ *Mary MacCrain's tombstone at Inverlussa, Jura.*

just two miles short of Kinuachdrach. Here, when very ill, he wrote his famous book, *1984*.

The west coast of Jura is a wild and beautiful place. Part of its charm is its inaccessibility. However, it is worth making the effort to walk over to Glengarrisdale Bay. It's a bog-trotting route so keep to the game trails if they lead your way, more or less due west. Leave the road close to the trig point at Cnoc a' Chuirn Mhoir, which is between the road and the coast. The distance is about four miles one way, give or take a few detours, and the bay can be difficult to locate in mist, so be forewarned. There used to be a gruesome memorial at the bay, MacLaine's skull. This unfortunate gentleman was slain in 1647 by the Campbells of Craignish during the Wars of the Covenant. His skull and bones were mounted in a cairn for all to see until quite recent times. The bay itself is magnificent, dazzling sand fondled by islets and skerries. Back from the beach is a whitewashed cottage, now a place of refuge for the Mountain Bothy Association.

There are various other ghost communities on the west coast of Jura, such as Ruantallain, whose headland forms the upper teeth of the mouth of Loch Tarbert.

Your soul will feel cleansed with a visit to Jura, even if it doesn't rain. There is a great deal to explore, more deer than you ever thought existed, and a singular lack of traffic.

Knapdale

RETURNING TO THE mainland where we left it at West Loch Tarbert, we come in our northward progress back to Knapdale and it is time now to explore it. No major highway penetrates the western side of South Knapdale, only the meandering B8024. It is worth taking this road,

---

The remote house of Barnhill, Jura, where George Orwell wrote ▶
1984. *To the north is the Gulf of Corryvreckan.*

either from its northern junction with the main road or from the head of West Loch Tarbert. The forty-mile route is well punctuated with views, duns and castles. Out on the west coast for example there is an interesting collection of sculptured stones at the entrance to Kilberry Castle. Above the front doorway is the inscription: "Plundered and burned by Captain Proby, an English pirate, 1513." (The castle, rebuilt in 1884, is not open to the public.)

Looking out over the head of Loch Caolisport is An Torr (187m/613ft). Ascend it from the minor road north-west off the B8024 for great views down the loch to the Isle of Islay. Conall, fifth king of Dalriada, and an in-law of St Columba, had a stronghold there called Caisteal Torr. Follow the road round the loch head and you come to the most important single attraction in this forgotten quarter, St Columba's Cave. This is located on the west side of Loch Caolisport, opposite Eilean na h-Uamhaidh (Island of the Cave). The road round the top end of the loch is lovely, quiet, wooded and in tune with the sanctity of the place. It is likely that Columba stopped off here while he set about obtaining permission from the ruler of Dalriada to settle on Iona. Then as now the real estate business was not easy. The cave itself is about a hundred metres above the road on the face of a small cliff. A stream nearby leaps down from a glen above to a clearing in which stand the broken remains of a chapel. Once there was a garden here, between chapel and cave. Flowers compete with ferns and red rhododendron for elbow room. The cave is about eighteen metres deep and high-roofed. It is loftier than it once was; a metre of soil was taken out earlier this century

Looking from the stream which was St Columba's water supply, over ▶
a rock basin to the ruin of the chapel and Loch Caolisport. St
Columba's Cave is just past the tree on the left.

The cave of St Columba, Loch Caolisport. Left foreground is the ▶▶
altar and on the rock ledge is a rock basin for washing the feet. There
is a further rock basin closer to the entrance.

and not replaced. There is still an assortment of rock 'furniture' inside: a round bowl hewn from the rock on the right, and inside the cave proper, a stone altar projecting from a rock platform on the right. You gain this by a ladder. A Latin cross is now visible, a small one, only seven inches high, cut into the rock. There is another basin cut in the rock on the platform. This was most likely for washing the feet, and the other for the hands before Mass.

Beyond Ellary there is no road round the western headland, the Point of Knap, to Kilmory and one must walk, or enter this part of Knapdale from the north at Crinan. This we will now do to retain, on wheels at least, a convenient sequence of travel.

The western section of North Knapdale is real fairy country. One almost expects dwarfs and wee people to share the lochside nooks and crannies and a lovely princess to descend from a shining tower. The area is most complex, especially round the head of Loch Sween, where fingers of this sea loch push their way gently into the carpet of the Knapdale Forest, and where boats using the Crinan Canal are seen as an almost arm's-length foreground to the vast expanse of the Moine Mhor, an area rich in the stone circles and standing stones of prehistory.

To explore the area west of Loch Sween, take the Tayvallich fork a short way south of Bellanoch. In less than half a mile along the western shore of Loch Coille-Bharr the B8025 doglegs north while a forest road continues down the loch. Leave the car here, and take the dirt road on for over a mile to a further fork. Keep to the left and in about a mile you drop to the pine-fringed shore of an abbreviated forefinger of upper Loch Sween. Ahead, the Fairy Isles, a flotilla of seven idyllic islets, are lazily patrolled by duck and oystercatchers. You can also reach the Fairy Isles by hiring a boat from Tayvallich.

A network of roads interlace Knapdale Forest and many fine walks can be enjoyed with enticing glimpses of birdlife and water. In the lagoons oysters are farmed commercially.

Tayvallich is a sleepy little village curled round its sheltered bay. Popular both with discriminating tourists and yachtspeople, it is an ideal place for base camp when exploring the peninsula. There is much to see and Knapdale's natural treasures should be savoured at leisure, not in a rapid motorised dash-and-done sortie.

From here there are a score of walks to choose from, as a glance at the OS map will show. From Carsaig Bay, on the western side of the isthmus where there is a sparkling beach, a track goes northwards for three miles to the old farm of Dounie, where the poet Thomas Campbell lived. The spit of land to the south of Tayvallich, in which Lochan Taynish is held captive, offers various gentle perambulations, each with its own peculiar charm.

As one goes southwards on the peninsula (on a diminutive strip of tarmac), the country becomes more stark and the shelter of the lagoons and mother Forestry Commission is left behind. One feels that sterner country is ahead and where better to have an outpost of Christianity?

Keills Chapel is near the end of the road and is opposite the Isle of Danna. The chapel is built on a ledge on the hillside just beyond the end of the surfaced road and is supposed to have been dedicated to St Columba. Behind it is a cross. The original cross and other stones are now housed within the chapel. This is one of the best collections of stone slabs and carvings in Argyllshire, now under the protection of the Department of the Environment. Buried here is Lame John MacDougall of Lorne, who was a deadly foe of both Wallace and Bruce.

There are one or two other items of interest in the immediate neighbourhood. On a raised beach across Loch na Cille, about 500 metres from New Ulva, is the site of an ancient settlement with stone cists and burial enclosures. Just beyond this, a causeway leads to Danna Island. The island is worth visiting for its views; there is an air of freedom about it—those more unkind would call it desolation. At the last outpost, the farm of Danna na Cloiche is said to have been built on the remains of a three-storeyed fortress called the Castle of the Red-haired Maiden. Two

miles south-west of Danna lies Eilean Mor MacCormack, a holy island with the ruins of a chapel, once the mother church of Knapdale. This was the church of Carmaig or Cormack. There are many interesting relics here and the chapel was used as an inn (with scant custom, I fear) after 1600. The south-east end of the island boasts a cave, the home for a while (according to tradition) of St Abba, a predecessor of Carmaig. The demise of the inn may have something to do with the haunted galley that appears from time to time with a black sail, whose crew were massacred by a holy anchorite! That privateer who made good in America, John Paul Jones, obviously unaffected by the ghostly birlin, landed here in 1799.

The track beyond Keills Chapel winds past pinnacles of slate looking like rocket launchers, and by the pensioned-off farm of Keillmore, to the old piers which were at one time used by drovers ferrying cattle from Jura. The dignified dry stone construction of the jetties is reminiscent of Inca stonework on a small scale, so perfectly do the stones intermesh. Without a grain of cement, they have withstood the wrath of the Atlantic for centuries. Also, if you have time, take a stroll out to the pencil of land, Rubha na Cille, which, like an unbelieving bather, reaches with a timid toe into that illusive gulf stream, now fashionably referred to as the Atlantic Drift.

The road down the east coast of Loch Sween is another dead-end, narrow, but bountiful in views. The regimented green sentinels of the Forestry Commission crowd it in for quite a way, but eventually you shake off the billiard table feeling and emerge on the naked coast near Castle Sween.

◀ *Inside Keills Chapel.*

The superb stonework of the jetty beyond Keills Chapel. From here a ▶
ferry used to carry cattle from Jura to the mainland markets.

Castle Sween, on Loch Sween, Knapdale. This is the earliest stone ▶ ▶
castle in Scotland, built in the twelfth century.

The route seems as popular with eider ducks as tourists and many of them, that is the ducks, can be seen paddling close to the rocky shore.

Castle Sween, Castle of the Warriors, is the earliest stone castle in Scotland, and was probably built by Somerled in about 1100. MacMillan's Tower, on the west side when viewed from the shore, has phallic connotations and here there is a fine marriage of stone to base rock. On a high floor within the tower there is a hole down which prisoners could be dropped to the base of a smooth-walled pit, the only exit from this being a drain going through the wall to the rocks below. The castle is of similar design to another Lord of the Isles fortress, Castle Claig on Am Fraoch Eilean where the Sound of Islay joins the Sound of Jura. The total floor area of the keep was a kitchen, so one must assume that the Lords of the Isles were real trencher-men. An oven still survives. The final chapter in Castle Sween's long history came in 1644 when Young Colkitto, the headstrong lieutenant of Montrose, lay siege to it and burned it and the Campbells out. Due to the danger of falling masonry, you cannot now enter the castle which, like all the best castles these days, is adopted by the Ministry of the Environment. There is now a tourist complex at Castle Sween, which is not too offensive to the discerning eye.

Beyond, close to the Point of Knap, is the tiny village of Kilmory, renowned for its chapel of St Maelrubha and the fourteenth-century MacMillan's Cross. The chapel is roofed now and looked after by the Ministry of the Environment. There are many fine carved stones in this collection and it seems a pity that the chapel stands in a setting which could be best described as a farmyard version of a devastated Hiroshima.

The road ends a mile beyond the chapel at Balimore, an isolated house. From here a private road continues, available only to walkers, through a glen where the crofters

◄ *The MacMillan Cross at Kilmory in the old chapel of St Maelrubha.*

were evicted in the last century. Like the Battle of the Braes on the Isle of Skye, the crofters of Stronefield gave battle to a police and gamekeepers' battalion and won the day, only to be beaten on a counterattack by reinforced police who evicted the people and fired the houses. The Highland gentry were a singleminded lot! The ruins are today a memorial to oppression and destitution in a once lush and fertile glen. It is possible to walk to the head of Loch Caolisport on this private road if some transport can be arranged at the other end. Otherwise a double journey is involved, but it is feasible to go to St Columba's Cave and back, or take in the glorious beach of Muileann Eiteag Bagh. Here is a five star bay, the best beach in Argyllshire and not a topless bather in sight. To reach the beach it is best to go via the ruins of Stronefield.

A circuit of Loch Awe

LOCH AWE AND its environs have a wealth of historical interest and walks for the visitor. It's an area of wild grandeur, well endowed with castles, forts and churches. At the north end where the beak of the loch pecks at the lower defile of the Pass of Brander, mighty Ben Cruachan (1101m/3612ft) rises like a strong man between Glen Noe and the pass.

The mountain is a good peak to climb, with wide views of mid and north Argyll from its tops. Some of the initial drudgery of the lower slopes is taken away by a Hydro-Electric Scheme road snaking up to a dam which the mountain nurses between its knees on its southerly aspect. It starts near the kirk of St Conan on the A85 and goes up to the Cruachan Reservoir (365m/1200ft). From here the circuit of the Cruachan tops can be done, eight in all,

Looking over the north end of Loch Awe with the summit of Ben Cruachan in cloud. The Hydro-Electric access road to the dam on Ben Cruachan can be seen rising from right to left across the hillside. ▶

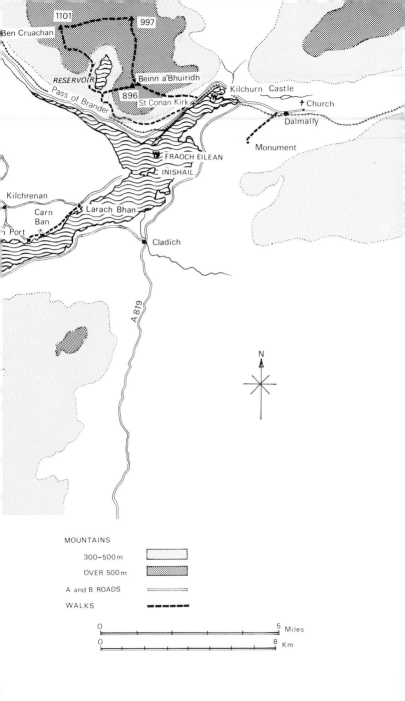

either by heading east to the first summit, Beinn a' Bhuiridh (896m/2942ft), or across the dam and angling up to Ben Cruachan, the peak back left in the left-hand corrie, Coire Dearg. Needless to say one has to have a certain degree of fitness to traverse these tops and a wary eye should be on the lookout for cloud and bad weather. From Beinn a' Bhuiridh one can descend to the dam, or slant down the hillside to Lochawe Hotel. This Ben Cruachan expedition provides quite a hard day and some hill walking experience is necessary.

The Cruachan Hydro-Electric Scheme is well worth investigating via its visitors' centre, for it is one of the biggest pump-storage schemes in the world. During off-peak periods the four great turbines have the ability to pump water back up into the reservoir with the surplus power generated by Hunterston nuclear power station which can't switch off when not required. The huge turbine chamber is an example of superb engineering and it is situated in the granite heart of the mountain. When the water is turned off, Land-Rovers can be driven up the steep shafts feeding the turbines for inspection purposes.

Close to the Cruachan Reservoir road-end on the shore is the kirk of St Conan. Built mainly of Ben Cruachan granite in a spacious Romanesque-cum-Norman style between 1881 and 1930 by Douglas Walter Campbell of Innis Chonain, it is architecturally unique and contains several interesting items. There is a great effigy of Robert the Bruce on a stone pediment. In the side of this, in an

The great generator hall in the bowels of Ben Cruachan, part of the vast pump storage scheme of the North of Scotland Hydro-Electric Board. ▶

St Conan's Church, Loch Awe, a unique building well worth visiting. ▶▶

Kilchurn Castle, Loch Awe, one of Scotland's most impressive-looking castles. ▶▶

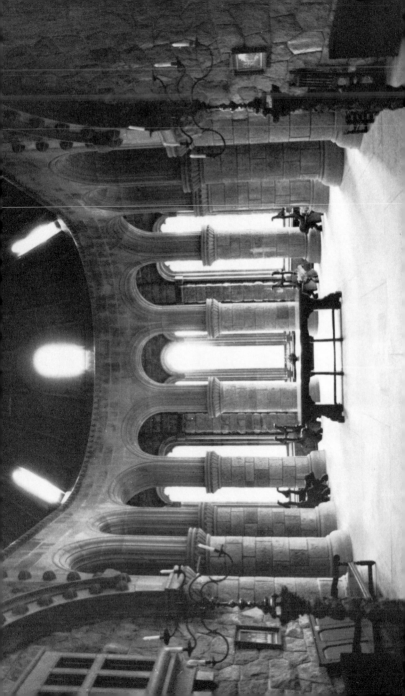

ivory casket, is a splinter of bone from his skeleton. The rest of that brave warrior lies in Dunfermline Abbey.

The Pass of Brander (a corruption of the Gaelic for the Sullen Steeps of the Torrent) has always played an important role in the communications of mid-Argyll. This narrow defile now carries the A85 road as well as the Glasgow–Oban railway. Sir William Wallace fought a successful battle in the pass, and here Bruce and his staunch ally, Sir James Douglas, outwitted the MacDougalls who lay in ambush for them. The ambush was watched by the elderly MacDougall chief, Lame John of Lorne, from a galley in the loch. Sir James got above the MacDougalls and pounced on them just as they were attacking and rolling huge boulders on the daring Bruce who led his men into the narrow pass, knowing full well they were putting their heads in the lion's mouth. The MacDougalls were routed and Bruce continued to take Dunstaffnage Castle and much of Argyll, which he gave to Campbell of Loch Awe.

At the north-eastern end of Loch Awe is Kilchurn Castle, pronounced 'Kilhoorn', possibly the most picturesque in Scotland. It stands, like a dignified but battered warrior, on a spit of land which was formerly an island. The castle dates from 1440 and was built by Sir Colin Campbell of Glen Orchy. It's only a half-mile walk from the main road.

In nearby Dalmally, a church several hundred metres north of the hotel is probably the finest Highland example of an eighteenth-century round church. (It is in fact octagonal.) At the cross-roads beside the hotel is Bruce's Stone, looking a bit like a surrealist impression of a reclining chair, where he is supposed to have rested.

A pleasant, purposeful walk can be made in one and a half miles from Dalmally to the draughty temple which is a monument to Duncan Ban MacIntyre (1724–1812), one

---

Probably the best example in the Highlands of an eighteenth-century round church just a few hundred metres north of Dalmally. There is a lovely stained glass window behind the pulpit. ▶

of the most renowned of Gaelic poets. His great loves were the deer and the mountains and Hugh MacDiarmid has managed to retain some of the magic in translation in this description of a hind from 'The Praise of Ben Dorain':

> . . . Volatile, vigilant there
> One with the horizon she goes
> Where horizons horizons disclose.
> Or lies like a star hidden away
> By the broad light of day.
> Earth has nothing to match her . . .

From the monument there are superb views over Loch Awe, and Kilchurn Castle can also be seen to advantage.

The road which continues down Loch Awe-side branches off at Cladich. Beyond, on the main road, the A819, is a further monument, this one to author, Neil Munro, creator of the *Vital Spark*. It lies on the west side of the road about two miles beyond the Cladich turn-off.

The islands in Loch Awe lying within the fork in the loch are well worth a visit and it is sometimes possible to hire a boat at Lochawe village. The largest island of the group, Inishail, was a burial isle. Islands were popular places of burial in olden times to prevent scavenging wolves digging up the dead. Inishail means Isle of Rest, and on a knoll there are the remains of a chapel dedicated to St Findoca, with an assortment of fine carved slabs. The chapel is mentioned in records of 1257. The nearest island to the north-east is Fraoch Eilean, still boasting some decaying tooth-like castle remains. The castle is similar in design both to Castle Sween and Castle Claig on Am Fraoch Eilean off Jura, and was built by Dughall of Lorne, son of Somerled, in the late twelfth century. After the battle of the Pass of Brander, Bruce gave the castle, which was previously in the hands

---

Inishail, Loch Awe, with its chapel ruins. Beyond is the defile of the ▶
Pass of Brander where both Wallace and Bruce fought successful battles.

of MacDougall allies, the MacNaughtons, to Sir Niall Campbell. The Campbells still own it.

Early legends of the island tell of a plan which went awry. A young gallant called Fraoch was asked to venture onto the island to gather the berries of eternal youth, which were guarded by that overworked watchdog of yore, a dragon. This expedition was not for his beloved, but for her mother, probably more in need of them than her daughter. Anyhow, the Celtic saga relates that her motives were not one hundred per cent ethical. Poor Fraoch died from dragon-inflicted wounds (perhaps third-degree burns), and the berries, which turned out to be poisonous, killed the mother. Moral: 'Tis better to grow old gracefully than to play with fire.

The road down the east side of Loch Awe is narrow, but interesting. At Innis Chonnell is an impressive islet castle, once seat of the Campbells before they moved to Inveraray. But for many years after this flitting, Innischonnell Castle was used as a prison for the Campbells' numerous enemies —that is, those they could capture. The infant son of the Lord of the Isles was taken here and here he remained until he was nineteen years old when he was rescued in 1484, in an SAS-type raid by the MacDonalds of Glencoe. It is not known when the castle was first built, but it was a going concern in 1296. The high curtain walls, nearly two metres thick, are surmounted by a parapet and wall-walk.

Off the shore, just south of the castle, is another island, Chapel Island, which contains a graveyard still occasionally used. Beyond here at Durran is where a hill track comes over from Furnace, Loch Fyne.

Still further along the loch, towards Ford, is Fincharn Castle, several hundred metres from the road across a field. Little is left of this thirteenth-century fortress today, other than some defiant stones of a square tower. It was held by Mac Mhic Iain, but later came into Campbell clutches. Allegedly, it met its end by fire. The arson was

◄ *Innischonnel Castle, Loch Awe, the original seat of the Argyll Campbells until the fifteenth century and used as a prison thereafter.*

perpetrated by a bridegroom incensed at the Chief claiming seigneurial rights with the bride, Una, daughter of one of the Chief's serfs. The 'house warming' took place during the wedding feast.

Just a mile from here, a short way up the hill path which comes over from Furnace, Loch Fyne, stand the ruins of an early St Columba church, once the mother church of Glassary. The footpath is signposted at the roadside and follows the edge of the forest with the church on the left. The ruin is fascinating and retains piscina, aumbries and font. Near the font, by the nave door, is the Devil's Hand Print, yeti-like and now difficult to discern. It has five toe impressions, three of these showing that he had not clipped all of his toenails. According to legend, a tailor was once working night-shift in the church for some unexplained reason and at midnight declined to leave his post when Satan dropped in. Somehow it was recorded that he said to the Devil, "I see that, but I sew this!" Which makes one wonder what old Nick was displaying at the time. Anyhow, the legend reluctantly reveals that the tailor ran out of bottle and fled. Though this church is in a depressing state of repair there is much to see, with many fascinating stones in the graveyard.

Ford is a peaceful little place with the hotel dominating the scene like a sergeant major. This was originally an old drovers' inn and a renowned fishing centre. An eighty-nine pound salmon was once washed up on the shore of Loch Awe near here, the biggest ever recorded in Britain.

Going up the west side of Loch Awe, there is an interesting standing stone nearly three and a half metres high on raised ground above a path at Torran. It has crosses cut on both faces as well as a cup-mark. On a small hillock nearby abutting the loch is the site of Dun Toiseach, where bronze artifacts were discovered in 1885.

The road crosses the river a mile beyond Torran. Here we find the Inverliever estate, at one time part of the

Kilneuair Church, Loch Awe. Just left of the nave door is a five-toe impression, said to have been made by the Devil. See inset. ▶

Campbell kingdom, now owned by the Forestry Commission. In 1499, the second Earl of Argyll, Colin Campbell, had the Inverliever Campbell boss and his seven sons attempt to kidnap Muriella Calder, child heir of the Thanes of Cawdor in Nairnshire. The earl wanted the one-year-old Muriella to be married to one of his sons, Sir John Campbell. This should have been a simple matter, as the earl was officially the girl's guardian, but Muriella's mother was not in favour of the match. All the Inverliever sons lost their lives in the action, but in the end, the girl duly arrived in Argyll. Miss Calder was obviously an heiress of importance, for she had been branded with a red-hot key by her mother, as well as having her little finger bitten off by her nurse as a rather heavy-toothed method of infant identification. Ten years after the kidnapping, Muriella of Cawdor took part in a forced marriage with Sir John Campbell. The Campbells are still at Cawdor.

Just before the viewpoint at Kilmaha opposite Innis Stiuire, a track follows the shore to emerge at the New York pier, about three miles along the coast (no skyscrapers here, only lofty conifers). New York comprises a house and pier and was named after the New York Building Company which exploited the Highlands after the Jacobite Rebellion by demolishing the woodlands of forfeited estates.

At Fiddler's Point (Kilmaha), there is the ruin of a small chapel, dedicated to St Mochoe, and beside the two oval-shaped ruins are two cross-slabs. Inscribed on a nearby rock is a Maltese cross and small figures. Above the road is the site of Dun Corrach. There are signposted forest walks in this area and it is possible to take the Forestry road from just north of the New York pier road junction and loop west then south to emerge on the council road again just north of Kilmaha.

Dalavich, an isolated village, is a community entirely created by the Forestry Commission. The branch road a mile north of Dalavich goes to Kilmelford, a scenic route passing by Loch Avich. At the west end of this loch, on an islet, are the remains of the Castle of the Red-haired Girl. She obviously played hard to get.

Running to the north and west from Loch Avich, opposite Lochavich House, is the String of Lorn track which, after some eleven miles, reaches Oban. The track goes to the north-east of Loch na Sreinge, and just past this is a cairn (Carn Chailein) to MacCailean Mor, who was ambushed and killed here in 1294 by the MacDougalls. Several hundred metres beyond, keep left when the track ascends right and go down by the Allt Braglenmore to the north shore of Loch Scammadale. After skirting this for almost half a mile, ascend steeply north-west over the shoulder of A' Chruach to cross the Eas Ruadh. Continue on a faint track to reach a gate. Go up the true right of the stream to pass a knoll on the left. Here the track is almost non-existent. Take the true right of the Eas Raineach, crossing two fords to reach a gate. Follow the path to Balinoe and Loch Feochan and the A816.

To avoid taking the A816 all the way to Oban, one can cut off it half a mile north of Glenfeochan and follow the small road by the River Nell. At the south-west end of Loch Nell there is a sinuous ninety-metre-long barrow known as the Serpent Mound and claimed to be the best formed prehistoric mound in Europe, where ophiolatry, the worship of snakes, was once common. When it was excavated in 1871 bone implements and charcoal remains were discovered in an underground chamber. (There are more Stone Age remains at Strontoiller, at the top end of Loch Nell.) Pass the Serpent Mound on the left and continue to Barranrioch where a branch road leads west to Oban. This adds about another six miles to the String of Lorn trek. As an alternative you can miss out the A816 altogether by going up the side road east from just beyond Balinoe to Kilmore, then reach the Loch Nell road by the north-west branch.

To return to Loch Awe, we have now come nearly full circuit. The chapel of St Crinan at Kilchrenan is worth more than a passing glance. Here, Sir Colin Campbell of Loch Awe lies, at peace we trust, for he is the unfortunate MacCailean Mor who was ambushed in 1294 by the

MacDougalls on the String of Lorn. His gravestone is built into the east end of the church. He was chief of the Clan Campbell and his castle, Innischonnel, lies on the opposite shore of the loch.

The shore from the North Port to Larach Bhan holds some interest with the burial mound at Carn Ban, a stone circle by Larach Bhan and, just north of here, two tumuli and a stone with cup-marks.

Also from Kilchrenan there is a walk to Oban, as well as a shorter circular excursion. Go west from Kilchrenan by a burn to reach a wood and enter this to reach Bealach Mor (259m/846ft). Here you can go south to take the shorter circuit to emerge back at Loch Awe-side at Coillaig. From here it's about five miles back to Kilchrenan.

Otherwise, soldier on past Bealach Mor to reach the southern end of Loch Nant. Part of the old path is submerged here. Keep to this shore line going west, then north, and cross the Abhainn Cam Linne. Follow the north bank passing Sior Loch. A mile or so beyond this, be sure to continue westwards across a ridge to the bumpy road descending to Glen Feochan. This in turn meets up with the Oban road at Loch Feochan.

Oban and north to Loch Etive

OBAN IS THE very heart of a vast network of scenic routes, by both land and sea. As a tourist centre it is ideally located, sheltered from the west by the great hulk of Mull, and the nearer island of Kerrera. From here vital waterways stem: the Firth of Lorn, Loch Linnhe, the Sound of Mull and the Sound of Kerrera offer seaways to the outer isles and the galaxy of other islands strung along this western seaboard. A large selection of boat trips is still available. Also, three main roads converge on this most important of Highland towns, roads which can take the visitor into some of the most scenic and historic country in Scotland. In addition, Oban is blessed with a railway link to Glasgow.

If Oban was known by the English translation of its

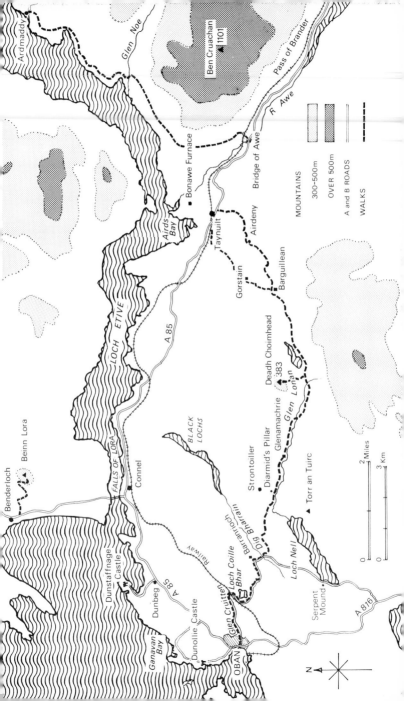

Gaelic name, Small Creek, it surely wouldn't have the same appeal. The bay is one mile by half a mile wide and the town clusters round the water, wreathed above by wooded hills and big houses. McCaig's Tower, a miniature of the Colosseum of Rome, looms above like a great colander, though McCaig's version is not quite classically accurate, being circular with lancet windows. You either love or hate this granite structure. It is certainly out of place in its West Highland setting, but it draws the eye with the fascination of a bullring. It was built between 1890 and 1900 by John Stuart McCaig, an Oban banker, with the object of giving work to unemployed stone masons as much as producing a personal memorial. The view from its seaward arches is worth the climb up Craigard Road from George Street.

Near the present line of George Street, the main street of the town, in the nineteenth century seven Middle Stone Age caves were found with remains of Azilian man (6000 BC) by quarrymen working on a low cliff a short way above the present shore line on a raised beach. In those days the water level was about fifteen metres higher.

There are three piers. The Railway Pier is the home of the Outer Isles steamers when they are in port; usually there are some sturdy fishing boats nudging this pier too, especially towards the end of the week when they disgorge their catches and the crews scuttle home for the weekend. The South Pier is the base for car ferries as well as being the yacht anchorage, whilst across the bay is the North Pier from which many motor boat trips are available.

North of the Railway Pier, Corran Esplanade hugs the shore leading up to the Dunollie area. Here on a rocky hill rise the ivy-enveloped ruins of Dunollie Castle, still managing to look regal in a beat-up way. This and the surrounding estate are still the family property of the MacDougalls. The site of the castle was used from very early times for there are records going back to 679. The present structure probably dates from the fourteenth to

◄ *Oban harbour with McCaig's Folly above.*

fifteenth centuries. The walls of the keep are three metres thick.

It was obviously a hard nut to crack, for it successfully withstood a siege by General Leslie's Covenanters in 1647, and also during the 1715 Rising, when the chief's wife, who was in charge of the garrison, resisted the full on-slaught of the Argyll Militia. The present seat of the MacDougalls is a mansion house close by the castle. This clan, one of the oldest in Scotland, can trace its ancestry back to Dougall, King of the South Isles, eldest son of Somerled, King of the Isles, who died in 1164.

Just a few hundred metres short of the castle, on the right, is the Dog Stone or Clach a' Choin. Here, legend has it, the giant Fingal tied his great hunting dog Bran, when he dropped in at the castle in the third century. The road beyond Dunollie Castle ends at Ganavan Bay, Oban's only sandy beach.

You can get to the island of Kerrera by motor boat from the esplanade, or by ferry across the Sound of Kerrera some two miles down the Gallanach coast road south of Oban. Kerrera is a peaceful island, a good place to spend a day wandering about. Horse Shoe Bay has a notch in history, as well as in the east coast of the island. It was here that King Haakon anchored his fleet en route to the Battle of Largs, and before that, in 1249, Alexander II also dropped his pick in the bay, sleeping aboard ship. He obviously had a troubled night, for next morning he told his nobles that he was visited by St Columba in a dream. The saint had bade him return home. However, the King rashly ignored this advice and landed to enforce his suzerainty on Ewan of Lorne, who was in cahoots with Norway. Shortly after landing, Alexander fell victim to some distemper and died before he could be taken back to his ship. The spot where he died is still known as Dalrigh, King's Field, close to Ardchoirc Farm.

Gylen Castle dates from 1587 and its name comes from the Gaelic Caisteal nan Geimhlean, Castle of the Fountains,

◀ *Dunollie Castle, Oban.*

for its two towers were erected close to springs. It stands on the south end of the island above a rocky bay, a MacDougall lookout over the southern approaches. Like Dunollie Castle, it was besieged by General Leslie, captured and burned; and on the insistence of John Neave, a Protestant minister, the MacDougall garrison was butchered. This was the same man of God who was responsible for the slaughter of a garrison of 300 at Dunaverty Castle in Kintyre after they had surrendered.

The Brooch of Lorne, which had been kept here since it was torn off Bruce's surcoat at the Battle of Dail Righ near Tyndrum, was looted by Campbell of Inverawe, one of General Leslie's officers. For two centuries, the MacDougalls thought that the brooch had been destroyed when the castle was sacked, for there were no survivors of the carnage. Eventually in 1825 it was handed back to the MacDougalls by General Sir Duncan Campbell of Lochnell.

Oban to Taynuilt through Glen Lonan is a peaceful walk of twelve miles on a quiet road. From the old parish church in Oban you go left down Glen Cruitten, past Loch Coille Bhar to Barranrioch. Take the right turning, then left at the junction of the track after crossing Dig Bharrain to reach Strontoiller and Glen Lonan. Near the schoolhouse in Strontoiller is a large standing stone called Diarmid's Pillar. According to tradition this is the spot where Diarmid O'Duibhne, a Celtic tough guy, met his end chasing the renowned Fingalian boar across Torr an Tuirc, the Hill of the Boar. Follow the road to Glenamachrie by the side of the River Lonan. Glenamachrie means Burial Place of the King's Sons. Children from the royal Dalriadic House of Dunstaffnage were said to have been interred here at one time. Here, too, can be seen a small Iron Age fort on the summit of An Dunn. Further on, to the left, is the modest peak of Deadh Choimhead (Fine Lookout). It lives up to its name, affording superb views on a fine day. It is not a difficult ascent from the river, but one should avoid the rocks. Beyond Barguillean there is an

◀ *Gylen Castle, Kerrera.*

A1 view up to Ben Cruachan and the road continues to Airdeny and Taynuilt. There is a slightly longer alternative from Barguillean which is superior. To the right of the Barguillean Nurseries cross the cattle grid to take a track north-east to Gorstain. This joins a small road leading to the A816 about a kilometre west of Taynuilt.

Just north of Oban, close to Dunbeg, stands Dunstaffnage Castle, still, after many centuries, an impressive hulk of stonework. Dunstaffnage means the Fort of the Seaweed Point. The eighteen-metre high curtain walls, still in a remarkable state of preservation, are three metres thick and stand between towers which buttress them. One of the towers was developed in the sixteenth century into a dwelling house and was refurbished in modern times. Dunstaffnage was another MacDougall stronghold (established by Ewan of Lorne, descendant of Somerled), until it was taken by Bruce after he came over the Pass of Brander, when he defeated the MacDougalls in 1308. But its history is much longer than that. Before the castle was built, the fort of Dunbeg stood on a grassy knoll near the head of the bay. Here it is said the Stone of Destiny resided before being taken to Kenneth MacAlpin's coronation in 844. In 1455, the last Earl of Douglas used it as a bolt-hole when he was at loggerheads with James II who had personally murdered Douglas's brother. The castle was also used as a base on two occasions by James IV when he was curbing the power of the Lordship of the Isles. Old Colkitto was hanged from a gallows made from the mast of his own birlin, or galley. He asked that he should be buried in the grave which was intended for his old friend, Campbell of Dunstaffnage, so that when the latter joined him they could exchange snuff. As requested, he was interred under the second step at the entrance of the Campbell burial area.

The castle was garrisoned by Cromwell's troops in 1652 and burned by Atholl in 1685. After the massacre of Glencoe, the nurse to the MacDonald heir was given

Dunstaffnage Castle, near Oban.   ▶

sanctuary here. Also that famous heroine of Scottish history, Flora MacDonald, who had fraternised with the Young Pretender, was held at the castle for ten days after her arrest on the Island of Skye. Part of the castle was destroyed by a fire in 1810. At 150 metres to the south-west is a thirteenth-century chapel where various Dalriadic kings are reputed to be buried beneath the floor, though these claims may in fact belong to the older burial ground of Cladh Uaine nearby.

Close to the chapel, a bizarre scene was enacted which illustrates that fact is often stranger than fiction. The Lord of Lorne had an illegitimate son, Dugald, the product of a fifteen-year love affair with a MacLaren girl, and in 1463 he wished to legitimise the boy, as he had no other male heir to the Lordship. This course of action was supported by the more responsible members of the MacDougall clan. However, there were other nefarious plans afoot and anything nefarious in those days could often be laid at the doorstep of the Campbells. This incident was no exception. The Campbells felt they had a claim on the Lordship of Lorne as three daughters of the Lord of Lorne had married Campbells, but they would lose their hold if the Lord of Lorne carried through his plan to marry the MacLaren woman. So he had to be stopped. As was often the case with the Campbells, they got someone else to do the dirty work, one Alan MacCoull, an illegitimate wayward kinsman of the MacDougalls. On the afternoon of the wedding, the Lord of Lorne emerged from the portals of Dunstaffnage Castle with a bunch of lightly armed friends and guests to join the bride in the old chapel nearby. On the way, they were set upon by Alan MacCoull and a well armed party. John Stewart, Lord of Lorne, was repeatedly stabbed and left for dead. Many of the wedding guests were killed or wounded, and the castle was captured by Alan MacCoull's mob. But despite Alan's efforts, the Lord of Lorne was not quite dead, and upon the instigation of the priest, was carried into the chapel and married. He

◀ *The iron-smelting furnace at Bonawe, Taynuilt.*

died an hour later, with his son Dugald now the rightful heir. But in the end the Campbells got their way and eventually took over most of the territory of Lorne.

At the Meccano-like structure of Connel Bridge are the Falls of Lora, called after an early Celtic hero, Laoighre. They are rapids rather than falls, caused by a submarine reef. It is an impressive tidal cataract, with thirteen and a half metres of clearance under the bridge at high water.

Beyond Connel, the A85 continues through the Pass of Brander, but before that, at Taynuilt, two side roads steal away to Loch Etive. Here, not far from the pier, is an old furnace called a 'bloomery' which is now an industrial monument under the care of the Ministry of the Environment. The iron smelting furnace was established in 1753 by a Lancashire company and was particularly busy during the Napoleonic Wars. It was closed in 1875.

From the jetty at Airds Bay a motor boat plies up Loch Etive, calling at various houses en route. During the summer there are sometimes two sailings a day and it offers a unique opportunity to see the loch to its best advantage. This service can also be used for the return (or start) of walks around Loch Etive.

Further east along the A85 at Bridge of Awe, a forest road skirts north and east round Ben Cruachan to Glen Noe and then a track follows Loch Etive-side to Ardmaddy at the wide mouth of Glen Kinglas. This provides a good one-way excursion if the Glen Etive motor boat is used. The distance is approximately eight miles.

Lismore and Benderloch

LISMORE LIES LIKE a large floating limestone garden in the mainstream of Loch Linnhe. Indeed, in Gaelic the name means Great Garden or, alternatively, a residence or fortified place. Take your pick, for there are duns and ancient monastic sites on the island as well. It can be reached either from Port Appin, where there is an inexpensive ferry, or from Oban where a ferry runs to Achnacroish. It

is difficult to see all the island in a day and if you land at the north end from Port Appin your range of operations will be limited, unless you take a bicycle. It could also be unpleasant on a wet day, as there is little shelter, few facilities and no public transport.

Most of the population live in the northern part of the island. Achnacroish is proud of a post office, a jetty and a few cottages; that's about it. The highest population density, a row of a dozen cottages, is at Port Ramsay on the north-west of the island. There are three castles: Achadun, on the south-west coast opposite Bernera Island, Castle Coeffin, on the same coast to the north-east and, opposite this across the island facing Benderloch, the remains of a tall galleried broch, Tirefour Castle. Castle Coeffin is now a total ruin. Achadun, built as a bishop's palace, has an unusual feature for Lismore—running water which gurgles out of its rocks.

Near Clachan, where there is a small store, is the cathedral church of Kilmoluaig, dating from the thirteenth century. St Moluaig arrived here about the time St Columba took over Iona, but he worked independently, died in 592 and is buried in the graveyard. His metre-long pastoral staff of thornwood is still in existence, now held at Inveraray Castle. The old cathedral tower and nave were razed during the Reformation and the existing structure, which is still used, is in fact the choir which was roofed in 1749 when nearly three metres was taken off the height of the walls.

Choose a good day to walk down the backbone of the island, taking in the top of Barr Mor (127m/417ft). You can start this excursion near Frackersaig and end at Rubha Fiart, the spearlike southern end of the island. The old track can then be taken back to the B8045 by Loch Fiart.

The remains of Tirefour Castle with the Lynn of Lorn, Lismore. ▶

The church of Kilmoluaig, Lismore. ▶

The name Benderloch means the Mountain Between Two Lochs: Loch Creran which sneaks into the backyard of Appin under Creagan Bridge; and Loch Etive, long, dignified and usually peaceful, a wonderful expanse of water, narrowing at its southerly end where it is spanned by the double piggy-back of Connel Bridge. Benderloch's western end pushes into the Lynn of Lorn like a disintegrating hammerhead, crowned by nine bays, but other than Tralee beach, in Ardmucknish Bay, all are stony. At the south end of this beach, close to the old railway station, are the remains of Dun Mhic Uisneschan, the Fort of the Sons of Uisneach. Some historians believed that this fort was Bergonium, seat of Pictish kings, but this is unlikely. The polygonal observation tower you can see on Garbh Ard across the bay was built in the nineteenth century. The bay below it, Camas Nathais, which forms the claw of the Benderloch hammerhead, is called after Nathhuis, or Naoise, one of the sons of Uisneach, a platonic friend of Deirdre of the Sorrows.

There is a path from the village of New Selma, or Benderloch, to the summit of Beinn Lora (308m/1000ft) of Fingalian fame. The cliff on the western aspect of Beinn Lora above the road was one of the portals of Bealach Bamruinn Fhionnghail, Pass of Fingal's Queen. The other portal was the sea.

On the minor road leading out towards the island of Eriska is Barcaldine Castle. The original building was constructed in the sixteenth century by Duncan Campbell of Glen Orchy; it was restored at the start of this century and the exterior is well worth looking at, even though it's not open to the public. It still has a banqueting hall and bottle-necked dungeon. It is interesting to note that the castle, now dazzling white, was at one time known as the Black Castle of Barcaldine. The Campbells of Glen Orchy descend from Black Duncan of the Cowl.

From the A828, the coast road to the north, the beech-lined B845 goes south over the shoulder of Benderloch to Loch Etive. Near the turn-off, opposite Barcaldine House, is the Kelco AIL factory for seaweed processing. Close by, too, is an interesting marine life centre and forest walks at Sutherland's Grove. There are further good forest walks on the south side of Loch Creran. One of these goes to the waterfall of Eas na Circe. A booklet on these local short walks can be obtained at the Forestry Office, on the B845, close to the main road.

When the B845 reaches Loch Etive-side the road forks. The left branch continues up the lochside for a way, passing the gaping dusty wound of Bonawe Quarries. This road survives as a forest road for some way and one can walk to Loch Etive-head after eleven miles. The lack of a proper path all the way may be well compensated by the sight of an eagle soaring high above the loch or red and roe deer on its wooded shore. Here, too, the walker may come across platforms cut in the hillside or in sequestered birch glades. These were used by the charcoal-burners who shipped the charcoal to the furnaces at Bonawe. It may be worth enquiring at Taynuilt if the motor boat service to the head of the loch can be used for one leg of the lochside walk.

Loch Etive-side was also the playground of Deirdre of the Sorrows, daughter of the King of the Picts, in the first century. When still a young girl, she was betrothed to Conchobar, King of Ulster. It was arranged that he was to take delivery of her when she was eighteen years old. She spent her girlhood in platonic friendship with the three sons of Uisneach, her particular favourite being Naoise. They used to hunt and fish and picnic by the shores of the loch at Airds Bay, or at the waterfall which still bears her name in Glen Etive. They had ten years of happiness by this lovely loch, the land of Cruithnigh as it was called. Then Conchobar's envoys came to collect her for their King. She refused to leave without her three friends and obtained a safe conduct pledge for them. But Deirdre's love for the three young men was so strong that she couldn't marry the King and, breaking his vow, the enraged King had the three brothers murdered. Deirdre died of a broken

Barcaldine Castle, Benderloch. ▶

heart a short time afterwards. She was granted her dying wish by the Druids of Ulster, that she should lie with her three friends. Dutifully, the Druids opened the grave of the sons of Uisneach and laid her to eternal rest. A song, 'Farewell to Alban', which Deirdre composed when crossing to Ireland, has survived the intervening centuries.

Ardchattan Priory is a mile or so west of the B845 fork on Loch Etive-side. The monastic remains of the Vallescaulian priory are incorporated in a later mansion. The priory was founded in 1231 by Duncan MacDougall of Lorne, near to Dunstaffnage Castle, principal seat of MacDougall power. Later, the priory became a Campbell domain. It played an important part in early Scottish history. A ruthless Irish mercenary called McPhadan used it as a base before he was destroyed by William Wallace in 1296. In 1308, Robert the Bruce conducted the last Scottish Parliament to be spoken in Gaelic at the priory. It was burned on at least two occasions. Today there are still many interesting stones to browse over, as the ruin comes under the care of the Ministry of the Environment.

Between Ardchattan and Connel Bridge, a path goes from Achnaba to skirt the east side of Dubh Loch Beag, then crosses the Abhainn Achnacree to enter the Barcaldine Forest by a stile. Here you go north-north-east to Achacha to reach the old road which takes you east to the B845 near Barcaldine. It is just over four miles.

Mull and Iona: sunken treasure, buried kings

MULL IS ONE of the most accessible islands in the Inner Hebrides. In places it is less than two miles from the shore of Morvern. The island can be reached via the Lochaline/ Fishnish car ferry or the ferry from Oban to Craignure, the latter being much more expensive, though more convenient. There are also further passenger ferries from

The ancient priory of Ardchattan, founded in 1230.   ▶

Oban to Tobermory and (summer only) from Tobermory to Mingary in Ardnamurchan.

Mull is a gentle island, embracing one with tranquillity, and there's room to move on Mull, for there is an abundance of empty quarters. The population is a mere 3,000 souls, 800 of whom are concentrated in Tobermory, the principal town on the island. This snug little port nestles in Tobermory Bay, a bay which holds the secrets of a 'Spanish' galleon.

The Tobermory galleon was originally the *Santa Maria della Grazia e San Giovanni Battista*, an armed merchant ship of some 800 tons, of a type known as a carrack, owned by merchants of Ragusa, then a city state, now Dubrovnik in Yugoslavia. Her captain was a Ragusan, one Luka Ivanov Kinković. In 1586, during a trading voyage to Sicily, she was commandeered complete with captain and crew by the Spaniards who at that time were gathering ships for their Armada against Elizabeth I of England. Some 300 Sicilian troops under the command of Don Diego Tellez Enriquez were put on board. During her Spanish service the name is variously recorded as *San Juan Bautista*, *Santa Maria de Grazia*, but most often as *San Juan de Sicilia*, to avoid confusion with several other St John the Baptists in the Armada.

Sailing with the Levantine squadron of the Armada, her crew in May 1588 consisted of sixty-three sailors. She also carried 279 soldiers and twenty-six guns. (Some were in fact not naval but siege guns, one of which is now outside Inveraray Castle.) Badly damaged during the English Channel battles, she escaped with other Armada ships round the north of Scotland into the Atlantic, only to be caught by the equinoctial gales. She was luckier than many in not being wrecked on the Irish coast but brought up at Islay on 23rd September 1588. She then moved to Tobermory Bay, probably in some arrangement with Maclean of Duart who held sway in both Islay and Mull at that time.

Legend and hearsay now take over, but there are records that show that Maclean borrowed some of the

Spanish soldiers on board to continue his feud with the MacDonalds and they raided the islands of Canna, Eigg, Rum and Muck, as well as sieging Mingary Castle. (Rum legend has it that their ponies are descended from Spanish beasts, and there is a Port nan Spainteach below Mingary Castle.) During November 1588, whilst Maclean was conveniently off on a further expedition, having borrowed two cannon and a hundred soldiers from Don Diego, the ship blew up. This was after a visit of one John Smollett of Dumbarton in the guise of merchant victualler, but possibly an English agent and likely in cahoots with Maclean. Almost all on board, including Captain Kinković and Don Diego, perished. Apart from the troops with Maclean, some fifteen survived, including several of the original crew who finally succeeded in returning to Ragusa.

Rumours of treasure on board probably started with Maclean who thought her to be "verie riche". It's unlikely he had ever seen such a large ship before. In the way of sunken ship's treasure—especially Spanish—these rumours have grown over the years, whilst the name was variously misrecorded as being *La Florencia*, *La Florida*, or the *Admiral of Florence*. Despite salvage attempts from the seventeenth century to 1982, little of value, except for a few cannon, seems to have been recovered. The wreck is in eleven fathoms of water and a determined effort was made to recover the treasure in 1955 with the assistance of Navy divers, but they discovered that the galleon now lies under ten and a half metres of clay. The right of ownership of the wreck now rests with the Dukes of Argyll.

Tobermory is best known today as a haven for yachts. In its backyard is some of the finest sailing in the world, with the galaxy of islands and sweeping tide races. Round Mull alone there are reputedly some 468 skerries, islands and islets. Before a major regatta the harbour is a forest of masts and the town has a festive air. Tobermory (Tobhar Mhoire) means the Well of Mary. The well is situated at the beginning of the Dervaig road opposite the graveyard

above the town. Though St Mary's Well obviously dates from early times, the town itself has a comparatively recent history, having been built by the British Fisheries Company in 1788. (Ullapool has similar origins.) During its more industrious years it boasted a population of 1,500. With the advent of the railway to Oban, Tobermory inevitably declined. Tobermory's Aros Park is now under the ownership of the Forestry Commission and is a place to spend a few quiet hours in an enchanting environment. Also the walk to the lighthouse of Rubha-nan-Gall offers views and gentle exercise. The walk to this point starts behind MacBraynes pier, then passes the lower entrance gate of the Western Isles Hotel to gain the path (there is a fossilised tree here).

Mull isn't short of bloody history and the nicknames of its makers leave nothing to the imagination: Murdoch the Stunted, Red Hector of the Battles, Lachlan of the Big Belly, Ian the Toothless. Just north of Tobermory there is even a Bloody Bay. This mile wide bay witnessed a sea battle fought around 1480 between John, Lord of the Isles, and his violent son, Angus. Angus was victorious and Hector Maclean of Duart, who commanded John's fleet, was taken to Tobermory as a prisoner in one of the victorious galleys. It was, however, a bitter victory for Angus, for whilst he was engaged with his father in battle, his new-born son Donald was abducted by Colin Campbell from Angus's home on Islay and imprisoned at Campbell's castle of Innischonnell on Loch Awe. Young Donald was held prisoner for fifteen years and Angus never discovered where.

It is possible to reach Ardmore Point (the most northerly point on Mull) and Bloody Bay on foot. One should take the Glengorm road which strikes off northwest from the cross-roads on the Dervaig road (B8073) west of Tobermory. About half a mile along this road, on a knoll to the right, is a fort called Dun Urgadul, the only vitrified fort on Mull. A little more than a mile from the junction, the forest track cuts into the depths of Mishnish, one of the wildest regions of Mull. It runs north and forks at Creag nan Croman. The right branch reaches the coast at Ardmore Bay, just west of Ardmore Point and en route, near the ruin of Ardmore, the track passes close to the shore of Bloody Bay. The other branch of the forest road goes by the ruin of Penalbahach to sweep westwards beyond a burial ground and thence to the old farm of Sorne where the Glengorm road is regained.

Keeping north on this road takes you to Glengorm Castle, a prodigious mansion built by a Mr Forsyth, a man who desired seclusion more than tenants; many families were evicted from this desolate parish in the nineteenth century. Close to Glengorm Castle are the remains of a stone circle and also standing stones. There are two forts, Dun Ara, a mile to the north-west, and An Sean Dun, the same distance south-west. It is about three and a half miles to Ardmore Point from the cross-roads west of Tobermory.

It is also possible to reach Glengorm Castle by taking the path on the western end of Loch Carnain an Amais. A branch, just beyond the fort of An Sean Dun, diverges westwards to the sea at Laorin Bay. Alternatively, some two miles north from Loch Carnain an Amais a left branch from the track takes one into the forest of Glen Gorm, and by keeping straight on at the next cross-roads, the forest road comes out at Dervaig, a hike of some five miles.

Returning to the B8073 at Loch Carnain an Amais, a path goes south from here to gain the north-east shore of Loch Frisa and can be followed (forest road) past Letter-more to Aros on the Sound of Mull, south of Tobermory. This is a walk of twelve miles. This path also has a twin on the other side of Loch Frisa which leaves the B8073 at Achnadrish and reaches a junction to the west of Cnoc nan Dubh Leitire. Here the left branch joins the Glen Aros road a short way past Tenga (take right-hand track). About a mile before Tenga there are standing stones on the left. At the Cnoc nan Dubh Leitire 'junction', the shortest means of gaining the Dervaig–Aros road is to take the right fork and gain the road just south of Achnacraig.

Dervaig is Mull's most picturesque village and boasts the smallest professional theatre in Scotland. Follow the B8073 round the west side of Loch a'Chumhainn, then fork right to the superb seascape at Croig on the Mornish peninsula. (There are boat trips from Croig to Staffa and the Treshnish islands.) It was here that cattle were landed from the Outer Isles, driven to Craignure at Grass Point, and there taken by sea again to Oban. Port na Ba, Port of the Cattle, is still marked on OS maps. Just north of Croig are the ruins of Dun Guaidhre and the track continues to near Rubha an Aird, a fine viewpoint.

Just before the scattered hamlet of Calgary, a road goes close to Caliach Point. The poet, Thomas Campbell, author of 'Ye Mariners of England', 'Lord Ullin's Daughter' and 'Hohenlinden', lived here at Sunipol Farm from 1777 to 1844. Calgary has the only shell sand beach on West Mull and it is a picturesque spot. From this point the Treshnish Isles are seen to advantage. It is a common misconception that Calgary, Alberta, was founded by emigrants from Calgary, Mull. In fact it was named by Colonel MacLeod of the North West Mounted Police in 1886. He had once spent a holiday in Mull with the Laird of Calgary.

The seascape between Mull and Ulva is remarkable and the coast is punctuated with duns, cairns and standing stones. Close to Burg where the road approaches the north shore of Loch Tuath, is one of the most interesting forts, Dun Aisgain. With still a fair bit of the stonework intact, it occupies a strong position on a precipitous bluff. On the cliff nearby there used to be a large eighteenth-century settlement. By the burn a Bronze Age hut circle has been excavated by a university group.

Torloisk is where Alan nan Sop, Alan of the Straws, finally dropped his anchor after a life of piracy. Alan, the illegitimate son of a Duart chief, was begat on a Torloisk lass during a voyage to the island of Staffa. As a penance, the girl was demoted to the status of a servant in her father's house and the unwanted, unloved Alan of the

Straws grew up to become a pirate. Upon retirement he returned to Torloisk, a man of means, and was a respected citizen, buried in honour on Iona.

Beyond Dun nan Gall and Dun Choinichean is the waterfall of Eas Fors. The stream drops from the left-hand side of the road, beneath the bridge, to plunge over a cliff into the sea. It is possible to reach the bottom at low tide by taking an easier descent route to the south, down a steep muddy gully—not recommended for the ungainly. Alternatively, several hundred yards on the other side of the waterfall an easy route descends to the beach via an old track.

From Ulva Ferry there are boat trips to Staffa and the Treshnish Isles (check at the tourist office in Tobermory) which can, in suitable weather, be memorable journeys in an enchanted island-studded sea. The island of Ulva was the setting for Thomas Campbell's 'Lord Ullin's Daughter'. The Loch Gyle in the poem is in fact Loch-na-Keal. Ulva is a privately owned island and for some 800 years was, allegedly, the home of the MacQuarries. The famous General Lachlan MacQuarrie of Jarvisfield became Governor of New South Wales and was known as the Father of Australia. His mausoleum can be visited at Gruline near Knock at the head of Loch-na-Keal. The MacQuarrie chiefs had the seigneurial rights of the first night with any Ulva bride, but were known to forgo this privilege for the gift of a sheep, which at worse raises some questions about the private habits of MacQuarrie chiefs, or perhaps just foretells something about the relative value of sheep and women in Australian society.

From the southern shore of Loch-na-Keal, Ben More (966m/3171ft) rises in prodigious grandeur. It is the highest

---

Dervaig, one of the nicest villages on Mull. ▶

Croig, Mull. It was here that cattle from the Outer Isles were landed and taken over to Grass Point near Criagnure. ▶▶

Fingal's Cave, Island of Staffa. ▶▶

mountain on the island and is the only 'Munro' (peaks over 3000ft) in the Hebrides outside the Cuillin of Skye. The mountainous area of Mull is concentrated in this remote central region. Geologically, Mull is unique, and the great lava beds form a vast array of terraces, a dominant feature of the island. In places the basaltic cliffs rise over 300 metres. Similar columnar characteristics can be found as on the island of Staffa nearby.

From the south side of Ba Bridge, a long but rewarding walk goes over the Glen Clachaig col (331m/1088ft) to reach Lochbuie eventually; a distance of twenty miles, but not for the weary of foot. Follow the south side of Loch Ba for two miles, then go up Glen Clachaig, over the Glen Clachaig col. The col is one and three-quarter miles due east of Ben More which can be ascended from here. From the col go south-south-west to Ardvergnish Farm, then round the head of Loch Scridain to Rossal Farm and up the Allt a' Mhaim south-east to the 396-metre (1300ft) pass between Beinn na Croise and Beinn nam Feannag. Continue east, then south-east turning the head of Glen Byre and the flank of Beinn nan Gobhar to angle down along the coast to Lochbuie. The walk can, of course, be terminated at the B8035 just beyond Ardvergnish, and the further section completed another day. An alternative route from Rossal Farm heads in a north-easterly direction to gain the A849 at Craig.

Opposite the island of Eorsa on the south shore of Loch-na-Keal the easiest ascent line to the summit of Ben More starts from Dhiseig.

Inch Kenneth lies in the mouth of Loch-na-Keal. It is

◀ *The mausoleum at Gruline of Major-General Lachlan MacQuarrie, first Governor of New South Wales and 'Father of Australia'.*

The road round the south shore of Loch na Keal. ▶

This boulder crushed the small house of a newly married couple at ▶ ▶
Gribun, Mull, on their wedding night. Their bodies were never recovered.

named after St Columba's follower, Cainneach. There is a fine chapel of the First Pointed period on the island which has deeply splayed lancet windows, together with Celtic crosses and sculptured slabs. It is said that Scottish chiefs were buried here when the passage to Iona was too stormy.

The road round the coast opposite Inch Kenneth is precipitous. The cliff face is the westerly aspect of Ben More and for years the road has been subject to rockfalls. At one time a postvan was trapped by falls ahead and behind. Gribun was the scene of tragedy last century when a boulder weighing thousands of tons crushed a cottage in which a couple lay on their wedding night.

A mile south-west of Balmeanach Farm is MacKinnon's Cave, probably the biggest in the Western Isles. To reach it you drive to the farm and walk south over the fields to a small gate on the cliff top. From an impressive rock flake a path descends to the shore. The cave is located opposite the necklace of skerries just past a waterfall. A hundred metres inside the pebble and sand floored cave a chamber is reached; this is about half way and now there is a right turn to reach the inner chamber. The cave was visited by the portly Dr Johnson who penetrated some 146 metres before he chickened. Earlier explorers were not so prudent. The cave was called after a piper, one MacKinnon, who volunteered to lead a dozen of his clansmen into the depths. Their progress was to be monitored by ear-to-the-ground colleagues above. MacKinnon and his dozen were never seen again. It is necessary to visit the cave at low tide.

The road now runs south-east after emerging from the Gribun coastline, cutting across the thrusting headland of Ardmeanach and the aptly named Wilderness. The latter

---

The route to MacKinnon's Cave, Mull. Beyond Balmeanach Farm ▶
look out for this rock on the cliff edge. A path descends just beyond the rock and leads to the cave beyond the waterfall.

The entrance to MacKinnon's Cave, Mull. Go at low water. ▶ ▶

Wild goats on the steep face of the Wilderness, Mull. ▶ ▶

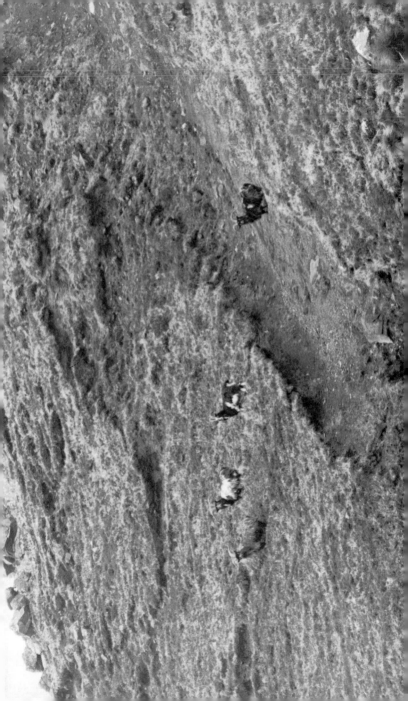

comprises a three-mile strip of devastation in the form of stone blocks, fallen from the 365-metre sea cliffs; an impressive place, but it represents a journey for the stout of heart, for the going is hard. There is a rough track (more suited for all-terrain vehicles), on the west side from Kilfinichen Bay which goes via Tiroran as far as Burgh Cottage. It passes Dun Scobuill on the right, part way along. Dun Bhuirg is about half a mile beyond Burgh Cottage. Beyond the second dun the path dips down to the shore and this is followed for about two and a half miles to a fossil tree, which is found immediately after a rocky buttress beyond two waterfalls. (They may dry up during a drought.) There are several signposts, one of these indicating a ladder, which allows access to the shore after a rise over sea cliffs. Just before the ladder there is wonderful, basaltic rock scenery on the shore. For those not up to the hike from Tiroran, or from the limit of their transport beyond that outpost, a visit by sea is recommended, though in so doing one of the most rewarding walks on Mull is lost.

The road to Iona, the road along the north side of the Ross of Mull, is the famous Pilgrims' Way. Near the head of Loch Scridain, a road crosses the peninsula to Carsaig Bay from Pennyghael.

Two miles south-west from the Carsaig Bay jetty is the Nuns' Cave. Useful markers for locating it are two large weathered rocks on the shore, about six metres high. The cave is just short of these. Here the sandstone was hewn for Iona Abbey in 1500 and there is still evidence of this work (stone for restoration work was also taken from here during 1974–6). The Nuns' Cave reputedly got its name from

Looking back towards Burgh Cottage from the path leading towards the fossil tree. ▶

Fingal's dart board? The route to the fossil tree is geologically fascinating. ▶

Interesting basalt formations en route to the fossil tree. ▶▶

nuns who sheltered here after the Reformation when they were banished from Iona. Old carvings can still be discerned on the walls. The Nuns' Pass is the grassy ramp, the break in the cliffs, just beyond the cave.

Just to the west of the Nuns' Cave, on the high cliff, is Gorrie's Leap, a precipice of sad history. It is said that Maclaine of Lochbuie arranged a red deer drive, and ordered one of his clansmen called Gorrie, if he valued his life, to seal off a particular gulch, so that the driven deer would be held up for slaughter. Despite Gorrie's efforts, the deer got through the defile and the drive was a disaster. The unfortunate Gorrie was castrated by the Chief in front of the assembled Clan. Gorrie was justly incensed but not insensible, and once set free, he grabbed the Chief's baby son, ran on to the high cliff face with his hostage and jumped down on to a dangerous ledge where others were scared to follow. He yelled to the Chief above that he would only spare his son if the Chief would personally agree to a similar operation with a dirk. Reluctantly, the father agreed, but even then Gorrie wasn't satisfied and leapt off the cliff, holding the baby. They were dashed on the rocks over 180 metres below.

The walk along the toes of the cliffs to Malcolm's Point is wonderful, for the cliffs here are 230 metres high, the grandest cliff scenery on Mull, perhaps anywhere in the British Isles. The journey is three and a half miles each way and boots are necessary as the route goes along the rough shore or on steep grass. Wild goats can usually be seen. The Carsaig Arches pierce the columnar basalt of Malcolm's Point. One arch is forty-five and a half metres

---

◀ *Examining the remains of the fossil tree, Wilderness, Mull.*

Looking from Carsaig Bay to the shore leading south-west to Malcolm's Point and the Carsaig Arches. The Nuns' Cave is beyond the point. ▶

The Nuns' Cave on the Ross of Mull, occupied by nuns of Iona when they were driven off their island during the Reformation. ▶▶

long and eighteen metres wide. The other sea arch is higher, but only a few feet in length. Malcolm's Point is a popular nesting area and the birds add to the attraction of the wild scenery. The first arch can be seen by negotiating the bouldery shore, but to gain entrance from the other side a higher path should be followed from the ruin of a lonely and idyllic cottage on the rocks. This path goes over the grassy top of the arch to descend into the sanctuary beyond. Here is a crazy thirty-six-metre rock tower pierced with a needle's-eye arch and to the left the yawning basaltic mouth of the main arch can be entered with ease at low tide. Care should be exercised crossing to the west side of the arch in high wind.

East of Carsaig a footpath also contours round the shore. It is equally dramatic as that to the west, with waterfalls and caves. It reaches Lochbuie in seven miles.

Further along the Pilgrims' Way down the Ross of Mull is Bunessan, which means At the Foot of the Waterfall. (The said waterfall is out of sight up the hillside.) At Uisken, where a side road to the south terminates, there is a crofting settlement, complete with white sand beach and skerries. It was here that the father of Sir Colin Campbell lived. Campbell was in charge of the Highland Brigade in the Crimea. He also led the famed Relief of Lucknow during the Indian Mutiny, where the pipe tune, 'The Campbells are Coming', was played by the pipers of the relieving force.

Before one arrives at the Sound of Iona, the road runs alongside Loch Poit na h'I, a favourite haunt for monkish fishermen in olden times. An islet at the southerly end has the moss-covered traces of a crannog, or ancient lake dwelling. From the east end of the loch a small road strikes

---

◀ *Returning to Carsaig Bay from the Carsaig Arches.*

The Carsaig Arches from the west. ▶

Nesting seabirds near the Carsaig Arches. ▶ ▶

north, past the quarrying area of Creich. The Victoria and Albert Museum, Blackfriars Bridge, and many lighthouses were built with the pink granite from here. Kintra is at the end of the road and the coastline offers some fine walks hereabouts. The island of Eilean nam Ban, the Women's Isle, is where St Columba dispatched females connected with Iona each evening, though nuns were exempt from this nightly curfew. The saint was heard to say, "Where there is a cow there will be a woman, where there is a woman there will be mischief."

Fionnphort (Fair Haven) is but a mile away from Iona and has an adequate ferry service. To the south of Fionnphort is the island of Erraid, famed for its sandy bays. Robert Louis Stevenson spent part of his youth here, as his family were lighthouse builders and Erraid an important base for both lighthouse building and staffing. A side road from Fionnphort goes as far as Knockvologan. During the summer months a continuous passenger ferry service runs from Fionnphort to Iona. It must be one of the oldest in the islands, having been operational for the living and the dead since the sixth century.

Iona, sometimes called the Cradle of Christianity, Blessed Iona or Jewel of the Western Sea, is the last resting place of innumerable Scottish kings and chiefs, and today still a place of pilgrimage, though largely tourist, and under the care of the National Trust for Scotland. Iona has to be seen rather than read about or seen on film. It *is* 'a jewel set amidst jewels' and Christianity emanated from here to mainland Scotland. One can still feel the strange powerful quality of sanctity and strength. The original name of the island was the Norse I which in Norse-Gaelic means simply 'island'. Originally, like so many places taken over by the Christians, Iona was a centre of Druidism.

St Columba was not the first saint from Ireland to land there, but he first established it as a headquarters for his missionary work with his Brethren of Columba. Columba

'Pilgrims' going ashore on Iona. The Abbey is in the background. ▶

was a tormented soul, having been responsible for the great Battle of Cooldrevny in which thousands were killed. He left Ireland heartbroken with a vow not to return until he had gained an equal number of souls for Christ as had died in that bloody battle. On 12th May 563, he landed on the southern coast of Iona at Port na Curaich, the Haven of the Oracle; he was forty-two years old.

The Abbey of St Mary's is a fine building of pink granite; for a time it was a cathedral when a Bishopric of the Isles was created in the fifteenth century. Standing near the west door of the abbey is the St Martin's Cross dating from the tenth century. To the south-west of the abbey is Relig Oran, a small chapel and burial ground. The name is possibly derived from Oran, the last of the Druids. It was in this small piece of ground that the Kings of Scots and of Dalriada were laid to rest, often after long journeys. It is supposed to contain forty-eight Kings of Scots and Dalriada (including Duncan and Macbeth), four Kings of Ireland, eight Kings or Princes of Norway, one King of Northumbria, one King of France, Kenneth MacAlpin, King of Alban, and Ecgfrith, King of Deira. The pirate, Alan of the Straws, already mentioned in connection with Torloisk, is also buried here.

As far as is known, Alan of the Straws didn't practise his piracy on Iona, but the same can't be said for the Norse invaders. Columba's sixth-century monastery was destroyed by the Vikings in 759. It was rebuilt in 801, but destroyed in 806 and as well as the building, sixty-eight monks were also demolished. This deed was done in Martyrs' Bay, some two hundred metres south of the pier. Once again the monastery was rebuilt and once again it was razed (825) and once more in 986. On this occasion, the warriors

---

◄ *The tenth-century Celtic cross of St Martin with the west door of Iona Abbey behind.*

The east face of St Martin's cross, Iona. ▶

Inside St Mary's Abbey, Iona. ▶ ▶

bumped off the abbot and fifteen monks. One obviously had to be a devout Christian to practise on this island.

Returning eastwards along the Ross of Mull towards the wide portals of Glen More, on the south side are Loch Sguabain and Loch an Eilein, connected by a narrow channel. Two further small lochs, Loch an Ellen and Loch Airdeglais, complete the chain running southwards. A path cuts off from the old Glen More road southwards, beneath the shadow of Tom na Gualainne, opposite Loch an Eilein. This track crosses the narrow strip of ground between Loch an Ellen and Loch Airdeglais, taking the east bank of the latter loch through Gleann a' Chaiginn Mhoir to Lochbuie.

On an island in Loch Sguabain the stonework is still visible of a former castle or lake dwelling. This was supposed to have been the castle of Ewen of the Little Head. In the sixteenth century a desperate battle took place between Ewen and his father, Iain the Toothless. Ewen lost both the battle and his little head and ever since, upon the impending death of a Maclaine of Lochbuie, a phantom headless horseman is reported to ride through Glen More.

To reach Lochbuie by road one must continue eastwards on the A849 to the Strathcoil turn-off and take the scenic side road meandering past Loch Spelve and Loch Uisg. Lochbuie slumbers on the shore of the loch which bears its name. There is a fine stone circle here and a rocking stone just over a mile down the north shore of the loch.

◄ *An example of fine sculpture, Iona Abbey.*

The graveyard of Oran where forty-eight kings were buried. Some of ► *the stones have now been moved under cover to prevent further weathering. In the background, Iona Abbey.*

The thirteenth-century Nunnery of St Mary's, Iona. One of the most ► ► *beautiful ruins on the west coast of Scotland.*

IRISH - STYLE CARVING
'FEMALE FIGURE
'SHEELA NA GIG'

The fourteenth-century Moy Castle—now in a dangerous state—boasts a unique dungeon off the banqueting hall. It is filled with water to a depth of nearly three metres, with a round stone in the centre upon which prisoners sat in total darkness and presumably did not sleep, unless they wished to drown. The castle is the ancient seat of the Maclaines of Lochbuie and is not open to the public.

On the cliffside around the easterly point of the bay is Lord Lovat's Cave, some ninety metres deep and forty-nine metres high. Below is a further cave reached from the larger via a narrow passage. Lord Lovat, who appeared to have had several subterranean hiding places in his time, was reputed to have been here after the Battle of Culloden in 1746. Unfortunately, the roof of the cave collapsed in 1980 and as the descent is difficult, it is perhaps preferable to enjoy the dramatic clifftop walk instead.

A road hugs the south-easterly shore of Loch Spelve as far as Croggan, a crofting community which also boasts a pier and a post office. A track continues for two miles round the mouth of Loch Spelve, and this offers a pleasant excursion.

Across the loch mouth lies Killean, a remote part of Mull, though there used to be a thriving crofting community at Gualachaolish until the twelve families were evicted during the last century. A track leads to Gualachaolish from the A849 close to the south end of Leth-fhonn. Just west of Gualachaolish is the site of Killean

◄ *'Sheela na Gig'—an Irish carving of a female figure built into the wall, Nunnery of St Mary's.*

The route from the A849 past Loch an Eilein, Loch an Ellen and ►
Loch Airdeglais to Lochbuie. On an island in Loch Sguabain, the most northerly of this chain of lochs, are the remains of an old lake dwelling, said to have been the site of the castle of Ewan of the Little Head.

Lochbuie stone circle with Ben Buie (717m) beyond. It is an easy ►►
climb up the south ridge (left).

224

Chapel. On the Gualachaolish track, a mile short of this old community, Loch Spelve can be gained by taking a stream to the shore. Close to this point are Maclean's Slipways, where the chiefs kept their galleys, and on an island nearby is the ruin of an ancient fort. Opposite to where the stream is taken to the tranquil shore of Loch Spelve, a track goes eastwards to Auchnacraig and it makes a circular walk possible by going on to Grass Point, then back west on the south side of Loch Don. This walk follows part of the very scenic Grass Point road. The crossing from Grass Point to Oban is the shortest passage and at one time it was used as a ferry point for the cattle droves (which were taken across Mull from the Outer Isles) and for Iona pilgrims. Close to the hotel at Grass Point a cromlech has been discovered and a further burial place at Port Donain, a mile or so down the coast, together with a stone circle. Beyond this again is Port nam Marbh (Haven of the Dead). It was here that the illustrious kings and chiefs of Scotland were sometimes disembarked on

▼ *Moy Castle, Loch Buie. This fourteenth-century castle, seat of the Maclaines of Lochbuie, is not open to the public.*

their final journey to Iona, though it was most likely used for temporary shelter, for it is two miles away from a recognisable path and across rough ground.

A side road from Lochdonhead, on Loch Don, skirts the north-easterly shore of the loch to weave its way two miles in to Gorten. From here it is but a short step to the sea with its complex of islets and skerries close inshore. Northwards again, about half a mile from Lochdonhead at a point where the road climbs sharply, there is a tall standing stone from which fine views are available on a good day.

One of the first close-up views of Mull the visitor gets when sailing from Oban to Craignure is that of the imposing Duart Castle on Duart Point (Black Height). By any standards it is imposing, both scenically and historically, its chequered history dating from 1250. It has nine-metre-high curtain walls which enclose a courtyard nearly twenty metres by twenty-four. The curtain walls are topped by a wall-walk and parapet with access via the gatehouse. One of the chiefs, Lachlan Lubanach MacLean, enlarged the castle in 1390 with a huge keep of four storeys and four and a half metre thick walls. All had been reduced to ruins, including seventeenth-century additions, when it was restored by Sir Fitzroy MacLean in 1912, the tenth baronet who lived to the grand old age of 101.

The present Chief, the twenty-seventh Lord MacLean, is Lord Chamberlain to the Queen. The origin of his clan goes back to Gillean of the Axe, who from all reports wielded it mightily at the Battle of Largs against the Vikings. MacLean's power was eventually broken by Campbell of Argyll when William of Orange forfeited Sir John MacLean in 1691. The castle is open to the public and is a must for visitors to Mull. The interior is a feast for nostalgia with its sea room, main hall, turnpike stairway, cellars, mural pits and prisons. Nearby is an old MacLean burial ground and a mile to the south is Black's Memorial, a tower-lighthouse dedicated to the nineteenth-century author, William Black.

Some two miles off-shore from this point is Lady's

Rock. The obscure landmark, visible only at low tide, was used by Lachlan Cattanach MacLean in an attempt to dispose of his wife, the former Lady Elizabeth Campbell, daughter of the Earl of Argyll, when he had designs on a later model in the shape of a girl from the other side of Mull. At night, Elizabeth was taken at low tide to the rock to await the tide and her fate. The following morning Lachlan was gratified to observe Lady's Rock sans wife and he sent word to Campbell at Inverary that Elizabeth had died, adding piously that he hoped her body could be taken thither for interment with her ancestors. Shifty Lachlan, accompanied by a host of mourning clansmen and a coffin, duly arrived at Inverary Castle. Lachlan was welcomed into the banqueting hall by his host but his digestion for the wake was ruined by the discovery of his wife sitting at the head of the table. She had been snatched from the rising tide by a Tayvallich boat crew. One version of the story duly reports his immediate murder. Another allowed Lachlan to return to Mull, but had him disposed of later in bed in Edinburgh by Elizabeth's brother, Sir John Campbell of Calder.

Across the bay from Duart Point is Torosay Castle, a Victorian Scottish baronial pile. Its gardens, which are of considerable interest, are open to the public. Beyond the castle a forest walk can be taken which runs parallel to the coast for about half a mile or so. A miniature steam train, 'Lady of the Isles', operates between Torosay and Craignure, which is where most people disembark from the mainland. The Oban–Craignure ferry plies at regular intervals across the Firth of Lorn. Further up the coast at Fishnish, where a car ferry crosses the Sound of Mull to Lochaline in Morvern, several forest walks have been laid out by the Forestry Commission. On round the coast towards Tobermory and half a mile east of the Forsa River,

Duart Castle, Mull. ▲

Looking across the Sound of Mull to Morvern from Duart Castle, ▶
with the Oban–Craignure ferry just above the cannon.

is the derelict chapel of Pennygown. Here one of the early MacLean chiefs and his spouse summoned the Devil by roasting cats. Inside the chapel is a very fine carved Celtic cross, alas broken. The carvings depict, on one side, a galley under full sail with interlacing flowers above and, on the other, the Virgin with child. Outside in the graveyard are many old and interesting stones.

Between the chapel and Salen is Mull's only airstrip. From Salen the B8035 cuts over the slender neck of Mull to Gruline at the head of Loch-na-Keal. Two miles north of Salen, across the estuary of the Aros River, stands Aros Castle, at one time an important stronghold of the Lord of the Isles. Its counterpart, Ardtornish, lies across the Sound of Mull on the shore of Morvern.

Aros was part of an early warning system for the MacDougall Lords of Lorne. From Mingary Castle on Ardnamurchan fire or smoke signals could be sent ten miles down the Sound of Mull to Caisteal nan Con on the Morvern shore and thence three times back and forth down the sound to Aros, Ardtornish Castle, Duart, then across the Firth of Lorn to Dunstaffnage and Dunollie. Using this beacon system, MacDougall could, within thirty minutes or so, be warned of danger on the western flank or, equally, ask assistance from his far-flung clansmen.

The MacDougalls of Argyll held Aros until 1308. Then Lame John MacDougall sided with the English during the Wars of Independence and Robert the Bruce gave most of his land and the castle to Angus Og of the Isles. Eventually the MacLeans acquired Aros, but they, like the MacDougalls, were a sept of the house of Somerled of the Isles, so it was more or less kept in the family. During Montrose's campaign, Aros was attacked and captured by Covenanting forces.

Aros Castle was last used for royal wheelings and dealings in 1608 when Lord Ochiltree held court for James VI. All the Hebridean chiefs were invited aboard the royal ship *Moon* to attend a service conducted by the Bishop of the Isles. But, after being wined and dined, they were all taken prisoner and bundled off to Edinburgh where they were released only upon agreeing to ratify the 1609 Statutes of Iona. Their promises to abide by these Statutes permitted urgent reforms on the West Coast of Scotland to be implemented.

From Aros there are fine walks which strike off the Aros/Dervaig road and these are already mentioned. The nine miles north to Tobermory offer some memorable views, and after three miles at Ardnacross it is possible to walk to the site of a dun, An Sean Chaisteal, which lies between the main road and the coast. There is also a standing stone on the high ground above the road.

Colonsay and Oronsay

THE TWIN ISLANDS of Colonsay and Oronsay seem at low tide to shake hands over the Strand, the interconnecting tidal sands. They are rich in everything to do with the early Church, with holy wells as thick on the ground as distilleries on nearby Islay. Columba was supposed to have come here before he settled in Iona, but due to the fact that he could still see Ireland, albeit only on a good day, he opted for Iona. Before he left he declared Oronsay a sanctuary for all time, and the boundary extended to half way across the Strand where, at low water, the base of one of the sanctuary crosses can still be seen.

Scalasaig is the centre of things on Colonsay. A ferry boat runs between here and Oban three times a week. Located on the east coast of the island, this village is easy on the eye, with prim whitewashed houses, gnarled hills and trees. There is a hotel and a post office, too. West of the village is Dun Eibhinn, said to have been the residence of pygmies called the Lusbirdan. Here too is the Hanging Stone, still with a rope hole in it, a grim reminder of sterner times.

North of Scalasaig, in proud woodland, is Colonsay House, an imposing whitewashed mansion of 1722. Both site and stones of the old Kiloran Monastery, dedicated to St Oran, the ex-Druid, were plundered for its construction.

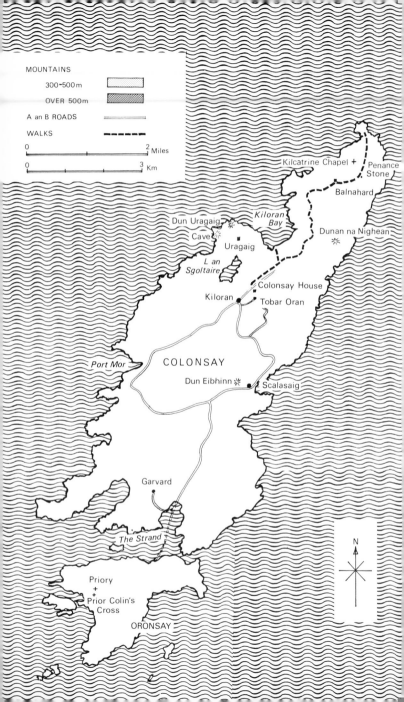

Little remains of the holy building, but the well, Tobar Oran, is still there. The gardens of Colonsay House are justly famous with flourishing subtropical plants and rhododendrons. These were well established in 1776. Kiloran Bay is a mile to the north, with a wide expanse of golden sand. But it can be a wild place in a storm. Behind the bay, in 1828, a Viking grave was excavated. It contained a long ship over a corpse and the skeleton of a horse. On the bay's headlands, both north and south, are raised beaches, and on the southern one, Uragaig, are a couple of duns and a cave. The thirty-metre-long cave is where Murchardus MacDuffie was murdered, in 1559. The original MacDuffie is said to have been a schoolteacher boss on Iona in 1164, and the name is derived from the glorious Gaelic Mac Dubh Shite, meaning, despite what one may think, the Son of the Dark Man of Peace. The clan had a magical coloured staff which could be set in a socket in a stone. Inland from the cave, on Loch an Sgoltaire, there is an islet where once a fort stood, said to have been a MacDuffie retreat.

It is relaxing to walk north from the Kiloran Bay track to the tip of the island. A bit over a mile north-east from the end of the metalled road, close to a wood, is Dunan na Nighean. This was a maternity ward for a wife of a MacDuffie Chief. Seven daughters were delivered to her on this site. Follow the track on to Balnahard Farm and then dare the further rougher mile to the tip of the island, known as the North End. On the way, not far beyond the farm, is the site of Kilcatrine Chapel, with a holy well used, it is told, by Columba himself. Near the grass-covered ruins of the chapel is the metre-high Penance Stone where nuns were flagellated, heaven knows what for!

Across the island from Scalasaig, about fifty metres

The broken shaft of a fine Celtic cross at the old chapel of Pennygown, Mull. Here one of the MacLean chiefs and his wife practised black magic. ▶

Aros Castle, Mull. ▶▶

from the road at Port Mor is an unusual meteorological instrument, known as the Heel of Cattan. This is a small depression in a rock seventeen centimetres by thirty-four, and only the MacVarich clan could conjure up favourable winds by giving incantations at the stone. (It is not known if this wind-inducing clan had any connections with the MacDuffies.) South of this is the golf course on well sprung machair, and near the shore is the Lifting Stone. In olden times strong men are said to have been able to carry it; modern man seems unable to budge it. At one time it caused so many hernias amongst the young men of the island that Lord Strathcona had it buried. However, it was exhumed some time later.

Chapels, ruined forts, and standing stones are at every hand on Colonsay. It is also curious to note that the diminutive road network is blessed with three separate 'A' designations: A871, A870 and the A869. The latter highway runs out of tarmac after a little more than two miles at the Strand. Here, at low water, is access to Oronsay. At the nearby farm of Garvard, there is the Hill of Pleas, a knoll bearing a solitary standing stone where justice was once dispensed.

Colonsay was the property of the MacDonalds during the seventeenth century until the grasping Campbells took possession. Now the laird is Lord Strathcona and Mount Royal.

Oronsay, as mentioned, was a famous sanctuary, and anyone crossing the Strand and passing the marker cross was untouchable by law. If he actually stayed on the island a year and a day, he was thereafter a free man wherever he went.

The island is fairly flat and protected from the often angry sea by defences of skerries. The priory, dedicated to St Columba, is a place of great antiquity, being second only to Iona in importance. John of the Isles, who died in 1380, is said to have founded it. There is much to be

◀ *Scalasaig jetty at dawn as the Colonsay–Oban ferry prepares to depart.*

seen and the prior's house, which has been re-roofed, now contains some remarkable Celtic carved stones. The wonderful Prior Colin's Cross is here, just to the south-west, two metres high, standing on a three-step plinth. This depicts Christ and dates from 1510. Decent burials seem to have been the done thing on Oronsay and Colonsay, for as well as the nag buried with the Viking chief up at Kiloran Bay, there is a horses' burial ground near the Oronsay Priory. If you have three days to spare you really should go to Colonsay and Oronsay.

Oban to Crinan

GOING SOUTH FROM Oban on the A816 the road takes a sweep round the southern shore of Loch Feochan; but before this, on either flank, the back country offers a variety of walks. The walk via Barranrioch and Loch Nell to join the String of Lorn track has already been described in reverse under *A circuit of Loch Awe*. Others will take you north-east by various forest roads to Connel and the Black Lochs; or south from the hospital on a circuit which leads between Lochan na Croise and Loch Gleann a Bhearraidh to Kilbride and on to Ardentellan Bay on Loch Feochan. A mile from Kilninver, a natural rock jetty on Loch Feochan is known as Creag na Marbh, Rock of the Dead. It was from here that many kings were taken by galley on their last voyage to Iona for burial.

From Kilninver the B844 strikes off to Easdale where a side road south takes you close to Ardmaddy Castle. The castle does not have an exciting history but boasts an eighteenth-century Palladian extension. However, an energetic track continues from the end of this side road to go over the hill to Loch Melfort to the south, and doubles back to Kilchoan and the county road. The distance is about three miles.

You get to the island of Seil by crossing the Bridge over the Atlantic, so called as it was supposed to have been the first bridge linking the mainland with an island. It was

designed in 1790 by Thomas Telford. Just over the bridge on the right a path cuts over to the farm of Camuslaich, at the head of Ardencaple Bay, where there was once an enormous and ancient fort called Ach-a-luarach. This was used as a quarry at one time and a gold bar and a sword were found. Beyond the farm, at the junction, the right fork is taken past Ardencaple House to the shore. Here a track runs south-east to the decaying molar of Ardfad Castle, an early MacDougall stronghold. To the west is Rubha Garbh, a frog-shaped headland. At one time the people living in this area were known as Frogs.

Back at the 'main road' again at Clachan Seil there is an inn called Tigh-an-Truish Hotel, the House of the Trousers. It got its name during the period after the 1745 Rising when Highlanders were forbidden to wear the kilt. Only enlisted men could, but not on their home ground, so this was a change house where they could don the less inflammatory trousers. This area was famous for its slate, but it seems a pity that those who profited from this enterprise were not obliged to tidy the landscape after-wards. Beyond, the road divides at Balvicar. The left branch goes down to Cuan Sound, and the right swings out to Easdale, or Eilanbeich, a tourist trap where the locals have made the best of a bad lot of slate, even succeeding in making Easdale attractive in its own way. The diminutive converted quarrymens' houses crouch below soaring cliffs. Easdale Island is a mere four hundred metres across the sound. It is accessible by ferry and the island's museum is worth visiting.

The island of Luing can be reached by the car ferry across Cuan Sound. The tide race through these narrows can run up to eight miles per hour. The island is renowned for its special breed of Luing cattle. Cullipool is the main village on the north-west coast. The Sound of Luing seems to breed islands. Probably the most famous are the

The Corryvreckan whirlpool from Scarba, with Jura beyond. This is ▶
the second largest whirlpool in the world, an impressive sight during a
flood tide.

Garvellachs, the four Isles of the Sea. The northerly isle is Dun Chonnuill, on which there is the old fort of Conall Cearnach, called after an Irish hero of the first century. Most likely it was rebuilt later by the MacDougalls or the MacLeans of Duart who both later owned it. Next to it is Garbh Eileach, on which there are a house and burial ground. Close by, to the south-west, is A' Chuli, which has a cell once used by St Brendan, though no evidence of this remains. Still going towards America, the next island (Holy Island) is the most interesting, with monastic buildings under the care of the Ministry of the Environment. On a small hill to the south of the hollow where the monastery stands, there is a gravestone said to be that of Eithne, the mother of St Columba. It is a small stone structure beyond the chapel, and closer to the shore are two beehive cells. There is a rock pulpit between the hives and the shoreline. Close to the north end is a remarkable stone arch called A' Chlarsach, of the Harp. If you have the time, try to get to these islands. There are boat trips from Cullipool and sometimes from Easdale.

It is sometimes possible to go to Scarba from Black Mill Bay on the west of Luing. Scarba's main claim to fame is the world's second largest whirlpool off its southern shore, in the Gulf of Corryvreckan between Scarba and Jura. To get there you have to walk, once you have arranged the return boat trip. Scarba is not the Garden of Eden, indeed much of it is left to the deer; though the island does seem to have been conducive to longevity for it is recorded that a woman lived on the island for 140 years, retaining her faculties to the very end.

The landing place when coming from Luing is at the north-east end and a footpath takes a line along the 120-metre contour to the bottom of the island. The location of the whirlpool is marked on the OS maps. The whirlpool, known locally as the Cailleach, or Hag, is quite a remarkable old woman and should be seen with a strong westerly wind blowing against a spring flood. The noise can be deafening and can be heard on the mainland at Craignish, five miles away. The tide race flows at thirteen miles per hour—the turbulence and whirlpools are caused by an enormous submerged reef. Many vessels have been lost in the Corryvreckan, though it seems unlikely that the fifty galleys of Breckan, the King of Norway's son, went down here. It was probably at a whirlpool between Rathlin Island and Antrim. It is also possible to view the Corryvreckan from the north end of Jura, but the main stage for the Hag's activity is close to the Scarba cliffs, where the great overfalls can reach over six metres in height and spout even higher. It varies in depth between ninety and 275 metres. Viewing the Corryvreckan in a spring flood makes one feel very small. If time permits, the ascent of Cruach Scarba on the return journey is worth it for the exceptional views.

Returning from our island hopping to the mainland on the A816, the turn-off for Loch Scammadale, a mile and a half south of Kilninver, is on the left. Here the shorter alternative to the String of Lorn track finishes. The loch shore is a pleasant place to while away a few hours, and for those with an appetite for the more ungentlemanly acts of Scot to Scot, it was here in 1644 that the spirited Colkitto burned alive all the Campbells he could find in the glen. This massacre was in a barn between Lagganmore and Lagganbeag and the ruins still retain the name of Sabhal nan Cnamham, the Barn of Pain.

From the Loch Avich road (which runs east from Kilmelford), a path goes southwards from just beyond Loch an Losgainn Mor to follow the west side of the Gleann Domhain stream to meet up with the side road to the A816, close to Barravullin, or alternatively across the river (ford) to Kintraw. The distance is in the region of five and a half miles.

Craignish peninsula is off the beaten track and the B8002, which gives access to it, meanders easily along the north-west shore of Loch Craignish, overlooking a flotilla of islands. One of these, the long barge-like island close to the far shore, is Eilean Righ, King's Isle. It may have been called after the Danish King Olav, who was killed at the battle of Druim Righ, close to the stone circle behind the

Campbell mansion of Barbreck, just across the main road at the foot of Gleann Domhain. The big standing stone on the way up Bealach Mor, close by the main road, may be where he was killed. There are the ruins of two duns on Eilean Righ and the large house on the east side of the island was once the home of Sir Lionel Johnstone, tutor to the last Emperor of China.

About a mile or so past Ardfern, on Loch Craignish, a side road can give a pleasant walk from Corranmore across the peninsula to Barrackan, thence down to Craignish Castle, a stroll of under three miles. But carrying on down the B8002 for about two miles, the wood-edged bay is reached which is the gateway to Craignish Castle. Across from this on a small hillock is the ancient ruined chapel dedicated to St Maelrubha. It's an interesting ruin with medieval carvings, large stone coffins and flat gravestones. Nearby, across the road on a small cliff is the ruin of Dun Mhuilig, an interesting galleried fort, well worth investigating. The castle, in its whitewashed splendour, is about half a mile from the chapel at the top of a small sea loch. Though an original structure dates from the twelfth century, the greater part goes back to only 1832. It was at one time a MacDougall castle and later fell into Campbell hands. It is supposed to have resisted a siege of several weeks by Colkitto in 1644, the same time as he roasted the Campbells in the barn near Loch Scammadale.

Take time to walk out to Craignish Point where there is the ruin of an ancient dun. From the point you can look over the sea channel of the Dorus Mor, the Great Door, a much respected adversary for yachtspeople. Though it is a deep channel, it is bugged by fierce tide races—up to eight knots. For astute navigators, there is a 'side door' in the form of an eddy. Here with a bit of cunning the busy main door can be avoided. It is from this end of the promontory that you can clearly hear to westward the roar of the mightier Corryvreckan whirlpool during spring floods.

Returning to Barrackan, a track leads north to Bagh Dail nan Ceann, Bay of the Field of Heads, on the west coast of the peninsula. Just along this path is a standing stone which has fallen across a small green mound on the left. This is the strangely carved Leac an Duine Choir, Stone of the Just Man, which according to local tradition sometimes has the power of speech. A fierce battle was fought between the Vikings and the Celtic defenders of Dun Ailne at the Bagh Dail nan Ceann, and two large cairns at the southern end of the grimly named bay cover the dead. Continuing north-east up the back of the Craignish peninsula on an intermittent track to the east of Dun Ailne, you reach a gate, beyond which there is a ford, hidden by trees. The way is now obvious to Gemmil and the Lunga Hotel on a minor cross-peninsula road linking Adfern with the A816.

After the A816 has swung east and south over the Bealach Mor, one reaches Carnassarie Castle, a good example of a sixteenth-century fortified house. It was built by John Carsewell, Bishop of the Isles, who had vacated the smaller castle at Kilmartin, a little over a mile to the south. John Carsewell was the first person to print a book in the Gaelic language, his translation of Knox's *Liturgy*, in 1567. The castle was built in 1572, but looks much older. It is in a good state of preservation under the care of the Ministry of the Environment. A spiral stairway can be taken to the top of one of the towers, and there is a fireplace in which a whole ox could be roasted. During the 1685 rebellion when Argyll supported Monmouth, the castle was sacked by John Murray, Marquis of Atholl. To the east of the castle, the B840 goes up to the south-west end of Loch Awe.

John Carsewell's other castle, Kilmartin, is just beside the road at the north end of the village. It is forlorn now and roofless, but it must have been an attractive structure in the sixteenth century. There was an attempt to murder Colin Campbell here, but he managed to escape through a burning out-house, after which he had to jump into the river to cool his suit of armour.

The village of Kilmartin is a happy little place standing to the north end of the wide expanse of the Moine Mhor, the Great Moss of Dunadd. The village is justly famous for its collection of medieval stones in the church and graveyard. The church itself is of no great antiquity, but nevertheless quite pleasing to the eye.

In the church is the famed Kilmartin Cross, a work of immense beauty, and a separate building houses a fine selection of carved slabs from various sites and various periods. Nearby in an open setting is the Poltalloch collection of stones from the Malcolm family. For those with an interest in medieval memorials, Kilmartin church and churchyard are a must.

The archaeological wealth in the area between Crinan, Loch Awe, and Kilmichael Glassary is unique in Scotland. Churches, vitrified forts, chambered cairns, sun circles, Celtic crosses, cup- and ring-marks, standing stones and monoliths signal the hub of Scottish history.

One of the principal sites of interest is Dunadd, a rocky knoll thirty metres high, in the centre of the plain of the Great Moss. Here, according to early Irish annalists, Fergus, Angus and Lorne sailed up the River Add to arrive at the fort in 498. It became the seat of Fergus Mac Erc and it is said that he brought with him from Ulster the Lia Faill—Jacob's Pillow—later to be known as the Stone of Destiny. Dunadd was the capital of Dalriada for about 345 years. It was an ideal site with good communications by sea and open space around to spot an enemy. There were also some seventy forts in a ten-mile radius of Dunadd for protection. Dunadd was taken twice by Britons and Picts during the seventh and eighth centuries, but it was retaken and was a base of Scottish power until the time of Kenneth MacAlpin. After he beat up the Picts in 843, he moved his centre of operations to Scone. You can reach Dunadd from the A816 by following the signposts. On a rock slab close to the top of the mound are three items of interest: the imprint of a human foot, said to have belonged to Fergus, first King of Dalriada, the carved outline of a wild boar, and a basin, twelve centimetres deep by twenty-six wide.

Also important is the area of Nether Largie in the low fields just south of Kilmartin on the north side of the Moss.

▲ *The Kilmartin Cross. The beauty of this cross is unmatched in Argyll, except perhaps by the Kildalton Cross of Islay. Until recent times it stood in the graveyard.*

Kilmichael Glassary Church. Though the present church is not old, it is built on the site of a much earlier one, with many fascinating stones in the graveyard. ▲

The South Cairn is one of the largest in Britain, over forty metres in diameter. The Templewood Stone Circle dates from the Bronze Age, about 1600 BC. The principal group takes the form of a ring of eight standing stones with a central monolith and burial chamber. Some of the stones are nearly three metres high.

Duntrune Castle, dating from the thirteenth century, stands on the north shore of Loch Crinan. It is one of the oldest inhabited castles in Scotland, at one time a Campbell seat, later taken over by the Malcolms. It is not usually open to the public. The castle has an interesting history; it last received 'attention' in 1644 by Colkitto and his Ulster-men, after Montrose's victory at Inverlochy. The Campbells

were at home and Colkitto sent his piper ahead to case the joint before he attacked. The piper was admitted, possibly to entertain the Campbells, and found the fortress would be a hard nut for his boss to crack. It had a very narrow stair that only one person at a time could climb. Somehow he aroused the suspicions of the inmates, was thrown into one of the turrets and from a slit or window saw Colkitto's galleys approach. Taking up his pipes he played the tune known as 'The Piper's Warning to his Master'. The words which were added later run:

> Coll, my beloved, avoid the tower, avoid the dun,
> Coll, my beloved, avoid the Sound, avoid the Sound.
> I am in their hands, I am in their hands.

Many years later a skeleton with mutilated fingers was found under the flagstones of the castle's kitchen. For ages a piper's ghost haunted the castle but was eventually put out of its misery when exorcised by an Episcopalian clergyman in recent times.

◀ *Close to the top of the mound of the old fort of Dunadd are these interesting carvings: beyond the wild boar is the imprint of a human foot, said to have been that of Fergus, first King of Dalriada; the other carving is a basin, probably used for ritual foot washing.*

Gaelic and Norse Glossary

A	river, stream (Norse).
Aber, Abar	also as: Obar, mouth or confluence of a river.
Abhainn,	also as: Amhainn, river.
Allt	also as: Ald, Alt, Auld, Ault, burn, brook, stream.
Aoineadh	a steep promontory or brae.
Aonach	a height, a ridge.
Ard, Aird	a high point, promontory.
Ath	a ford, also a kiln.
Ay, Ey, I	island (Norse).
Baile	usually Bal, Bali, town, homestead.
Bàn	white, fair.
Bàrr	a point, extremity.
Beag	also as: Beg, little, small.
Bealach	breach, pass, gap, col.
Beinn	also as: Ben, a mountain.
Bidean	summit.
Binnean	also as: Binnein, a pinnacle or little mountain.
Bò (pl. Bà)	cow, cows.
Bruaich	a bank, brae, brim, steep place.
Buidhe	yellow, golden coloured.
Cadh	a pass, steep path.
Cailleach	a nun, old woman, a witch.
Caisteal	castle.
Cam	crooked, bent, one-eyed.
Camas	also as: Camus, bay, bend, channel.
Caol	also as: Caolas, Kyle, strait, firth, narrow.
Càrn	a heap of stones, cairn.
Carr	broken ground.
Ceann	also as: Ken, Kin, head, headland.
Cill, Kil	a cell, church.
Clach	a stone.
Clachan	stones, hamlet.
Cladh	a churchyard, a burying place.
Cnap	a knob, hillock.
Cnoc, Knock	a knoll.
Coill, Coille	a wood, forest.
Coire	Anglicised form: Corrie, a cauldron, kettle, circular hollow.
Corran	a sickle; semi-circular bay.
Creag	also as: Craig, a rock, cliff.
Crioch	boundary, frontier, landmark.
Crò	a sheepfold, pen.
Crom	bent, sloping, crooked.
Cruach	stack, heap, haunch.
Cùl	the back.
Dail	a field.
Dearg	red.
Doire	grove, hollow.
Druim	also as: Drem, Drom, Drum, the back, ridge.
Dobhar	water, a stream.
Dorus	door. Deoch an doruis, a stirrup-cup.

Dubh, Dhu	black, dark.
Dùn	a fort, castle, heap.
Eagach	notched.
Ear	east.
Eas	a waterfall.
Easach	a cascade.
Eilean	an island.
Fada	long.
Fearn	an alder tree.
Féith	bog, sinewy stream, a vein.
Fiadh	a deer.
Fionn	fair, white.
Gabhar	a goat.
Garbh,	also as: Garve, rough.
Geal	white, clear, bright.
Geodha	a narrow creek, chasm, rift, cove.
Gearanach	a wall-like ridge.
Geàrr	short.
Glais	a stream, burn.
Glas	grey, pale, wan, green.
Gleann	usually Glen, narrow valley, dale, dell.
Gob	point, beak.
Gorm	blue, azure, green.
Gualann	shoulder of mountain or hill.
Lag	usually Lagan, Logie, a hollow in a hill.
Lair	an axe.
Lairig	the sloping face of a hill, a pass.
Leac	a ledge.
Leathad	a slope, declivity.
Leathan	broad.
Leitir	a slope.
Liath	grey.
Linne	pool, sound, channel.
Lòn	a marsh, morass.
Màm	a round or gently rising hill.
Maol	headland, bald top, cape.
Meall	knob, lump, rounded hill.
Monadh	moor, heath, hill, mountain.
Mòine	also as: Mointeach, peat-mossland, mossy.
Mór	great, large, tall. Anglicised form: More.
Muileann	mill.
Muir	the sea.
Mullach	a rounded hill.
Rathad	a road, way.
Réidh	plain, level, smooth.
Riabhach	also as: Riach, drab, greyish, brindled, grizzled.
Righ	king.
Roinn	a point, headland, peninsula.
Ros, Ross	a point, promontory.

Ruadh	red, reddish.
Rudha	usually Ru, Rhu, Row, promontory.
Sean	old, aged, ancient.
Sgorr	also as: Sgurr, Scaur, a peak, conical sharp rock.
Sgreamach	rocky.
Sith	a fairy. Sithean, a fairy hillock or knoll.
Sneachd	snow.
Srath, Strath	a wide valley, plain beside a river.
Sròn, Strone	nose, peak, promontory.
Sruth, Struan	a stream, current.
Stac	a steep rock, conical hill (Norse).
Stob	a point.
Stùc	a pinnacle, peak, conical steep rock.
Suidhe	sitting, resting place.
Taigh, Tigh	usually Tay, Ty, a house.
Teallach	a forge.
Tìr, Tyr	country, region, land.
Tobar	a well, spring, fountain.
Toll	a hole.
Tom	a hilloch, mound.
Tòrr	a mound, heap, hill.
Tulach	knoll, hillock, eminence. Anglicised forms: Tilly, Tully, Tulloch.
Uachdar	usually Auchter, Ochter, upper land.
Uaine	green.
Uamh	a cave, grave.
Uig	a nook, bay.
Uisge	water, rain.

Index

Map references are given in italic, **pictures in bold type**